D1091835

CONTENTS

BASICS

XBOX 360 CONTROLS

Button	Command
LT	Aim Down Sight (ADS)
RT	Fire Weapon
LB	Throw Secondary
RB	Throw Primary
Y	Switch Weapons
X	Reload/Use
B	Crouch/Stand
A	Vault/Climb
R	Aim/Look (Click to Melee)
L	Move/Strafe (Click to Sprint)
↓	Toggle Smartphone
←	Weapon Attachment
↑	Nightvision
BACK	Scoreboard (MP only)
START	Pause Menu/Objectives

PLAYSTATION 3 CONTROLS

Button	Command
L2	Aim Down Sight (ADS)
R2	Fire Weapon
L1	Throw Secondary
R1	Throw Primary
△	Switch Weapon
□	Reload/Use
○	Crouch/Stand
✕	Vault/Climb
Right Control Stick	Aim/Look (Click to Melee)
Left Control Stick	Move/Strafe (Click to Sprint)
✛	Toggle Smartphone
✛	Weapon Attachment
✛	Nightvision
SELECT	Scoreboard (MP Only)
Start	Objectives/Menu

PLAYSTATION MOVE CONTROLLER

Button	Command
□	Vault/Climb
✕	Crouch/Stand
△	Switch Weapon
○	Throw Primary
Move	Use/Reload
SELECT	Scoreboard (MP only)
Start	Objectives/Menu
Control Stick	Move/Strafe (L3 button to Sprint/Lock Camera)
L1	Melee
L2	Aim Down Sight (ADS)
✛	Toggle Smartphone
✛	Weapon Attachment
✛	Nightvision/Throw Secondary

GAMEPLAY MODES

There are three gameplay modes in *GoldenEye 007: Reloaded*, they are: Single Player, M16 OPS, and Multiplayer. Below is a brief description of the main features in these modes.

4

SINGLE PLAYER CAMPAIGN

The Single Player Campaign is the subject of our walkthrough. There are four difficulty levels within the Single Player Campaign:

 **OPERATIVE**

 **007**

AGENT

007 CLASSIC

To complete a level on Operative you must simply get to the end of the level. On other difficulties you're typically required to complete secondary objectives, such as taking photographs or obtaining data by hacking with the smartphone.

Difficulty level also affects some game-wide parameters. With a higher difficulty setting the following can be expected: AI throws grenades more often, AI stays in cover more, and you have less health.

007 Classic is identical to 007 except it uses non-regenerative health, and there are body Armor power-ups. This health system mirrors the original GoldenEye 007.

SECONDARY OBJECTIVES

Secondary Objectives are featured in many missions, but if you play on Operative difficulty (Easy) then you don't see these objectives. The mission won't be *"complete"* unless you have completed all the secondary objectives.

Achievements and Trophies are the reward for completing all secondary objectives per level. If you fail to find all the secondary objectives, you are still allowed to progress to the next level on the same difficulty setting.

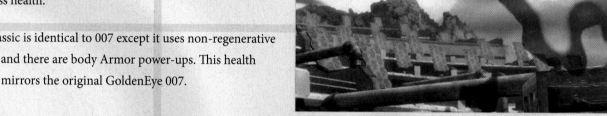

MI6 OPS: CHALLENGE LEVELS

There are 11 MI6 Ops levels. Locked levels are unlocked by earning stars, which are rewarded for completing these MI6 Ops levels. Levels are unlocked in the following groups:

Level Set Unlock Requirement

Level Range	Stars Need for Unlock
Levels 1-3	0 Stars
Levels 4-6	4 Stars
Levels 7-9	10 Stars
Level 10-11	20 Stars

MI6 Ops levels do not have a score or a time limit and do not have checkpoints. If you die, you must restart the mission. The challenge is to simply complete the level without dying.

Note that Stars are awarded depending on the player's score. The score is influenced by the difficulty rating and the amount of time it takes the player to complete a mission. The higher the difficulty rating, the higher the possible score. For example, setting player health to lower values and turning up enemy health and aggression will increase the difficulty rating.

MI6 OPS LEVELS

Level	Type	Description
Jungle	Elimination	Eliminate all hostiles in the area as quickly as possible.
Memorial	Defense	Defend 3 consoles from enemy attacks while you download the data.
Station	Stealth	Eliminate all hostiles in the level covertly.
Nightclub	Elimination	Eliminate all hostiles in the area as quickly as possible.
Docks	Defense	Defend 3 consoles from enemy attacks while you download the data.
Airfield	Stealth	Eliminate all hostiles in the level covertly.
Facility	Elimination	Eliminate all hostiles in the area as quickly as possible.
Outpost	Defense	Defend 3 consoles from enemy attacks while you download the data.
Archives	Elimination	Eliminate all hostiles in the area as quickly as possible.
Nightclub	Stealth	Eliminate all hostiles in the level covertly.
Solar	Assault	Reach the extraction point without getting killed.

MI6 OPS MISSION OPTIONS

These MI6 Ops mission options modify the single player experience by making it easier or harder, funnier, or very serious. The following is a list of all the options, and how you can further tweak an option. We've also included a description and how the option is unlocked.

Option Name	Selection Choices	Description	Unlock
Player Health	1% to 100%	Scale the health of the player.	Obtain Bonus Star 4 in Nightclub (Elimination).
Console Health	1% to 100%	Scale the amount of damage the data console can take before being destroyed.	Obtain Bonus Star 2 in Docks (Defense).
Enemy Count	30 to 80	Set the number of enemies that must be killed to complete the mission.	Complete the Single Player Story campaign (on any difficulty).
Enemy Health	1% to 100%	Scale the health of the enemies.	Obtain Bonus Star 5 (Memorial Defense)
Enemy Accuracy	1% to 100%	Affect the weapon accuracy of the enemies.	Obtain Bonus Star 7 (Archives Elimination).
Enemy Aggressiveness	1% to 100%	Affect how often enemies fire, and how much they favor attacking over self-preservation.	Complete the Single Player Story campaign (on any difficulty).
Enemy Grenade Frequency	1% to 100%	Affect how often enemies throw grenades.	Obtain Bonus Star 8 (Facility Elimination).
Radar Mode	Normal, Dots Always On, Off	Choose between 3 different HUD radar settings.	Complete the Single Player Story campaign (on any difficulty).
Infinite Ammo	On/Off	All weapons have infinite ammo.	Obtain Bonus Star 10 (Nightclub Stealth).
Golden Gun	On/Off	Your P99 is replaced by the Golden Gun. It's a one-shot kill with infinite ammo.	Obtain Bonus Star 6 (Airfield Stealth).
RPG	On/Off	Your P99 is replaced by an RPG with infinite ammo.	Obtain Bonus Star 11 (Solar Park Assault).
Marksman	On/Off	Shooting enemies below the neck does no damage.	Obtain Bonus Star 1 (Jungle Elimination).
Paintball Mode	On/Off	All weapons fire deadly, multi-colored paintballs instead of bullets.	Complete the Single Player Story campaign (on any difficulty).
Ragdoll	On/Off	Enemies always get launched into the air when killed.	Complete the Single Player Story campaign (on any difficulty).

CHARACTERS

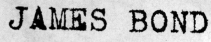

JAMES BOND

Agent 007 of the MI6 Secret Service, James Bond is considered to be Her Majesty's most secret agent. Dangerous, physical and aggressive, Bond owns a unique combination of skills with which to take down the most intimidating foes in the most challenging circumstances.

007

CLASSIFIED

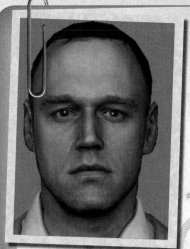

ALEC TREVELYAN

As Agent 006, Alec Trevelyan has had all the training and experience that being one of Britain's premier agents can provide. A close friend of Bond, his help has proved invaluable time and time again. As Bond works to tighten the noose around the Janus crime syndicate, Alec Trevelyan proves to be much more than he seems.

NATALYA SIMONOVA

A Level Two missile guidance systems programmer at Severnaya facility, Natalya becomes the sole survivor after the attack on the facility. With her skills, she soon becomes a much sought after asset.

M

M is the head of the British Secret Intelligence Service (MI6). Bond is her number one agent.

BILL TANNER

Bill Tanner, MI6's Chief Of Staff. Works very closely with M, assisting Bond's missions.

XENIA ONATOPP

Xenia, born in the former Soviet Republic of Georgia, was a fighter pilot in the Red Air Force. She is a classic "femme fatale" and draws sexual fulfillment from killing. After the fall of the USSR, she joined the Janus crime syndicate where she can put her various skills to use.

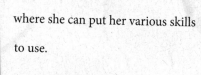

ARKADY OURUMOV

General Ourumov joined the Soviet Army when he was just eighteen years old. He always had a passion for power and used whatever means necessary to get his way. Twenty-seven years later, Ourumov had been promoted to Colonel and headed up a Soviet Russian Chemical Weapons Factory. When the leader of Janus offered Ourumov a part in his plan, the newly minted general graciously accepted…for the right price.

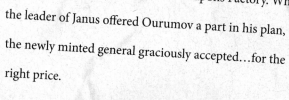

VALENTIN ZUKOVSKY

Ex-KGB agent, Valentin Dmitrovich Zukovsky, is a busy man. He has close connections with the Russian mafia, operates a bar, a casino, and manages a caviar factory. Bond once shot him in the leg while Valentin served as a KGB agent. Zukovsky now limps because of Bond, but his help is invaluable, even if it is forced out of him with a PPK.

DMITRI MISHKIN

Hardened Defense Minister, Dmitri Mishkin is tired and worn from the Cold War and eagerly awaiting retirement. Unfortunately, there's still work to be done and he agrees to aid Bond in finding evidence against Janus.

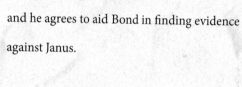

MULTIPLAYER

THE EXPERIENCE SYSTEM

Players track their performance using experience points (XP) earned during multiplayer matches. XP can be earned by making eliminations and completing objectives. As the player earns more XP, they increase their rank and are awarded new, more powerful weapons and gadgets from Q-Division.

MULTIPLAYER MENU

Access the Multiplayer Menu to compete with your friends online and offline.

ONLINE: Play online with up to 16 players.

SPLIT SCREEN: Play with up to three friends on one console.

16

LOCAL SPLIT SCREEN GAME MODES

CONFLICT

In Conflict there are no teams, no friends and only one rule: kill as many enemies as you can as fast as you can. The player with the highest score is the winner.

GOLDEN GUN

This mode offers Conflict style gameplay with a special weapon to locate and use. The Golden Gun is a one-shot kill at any range and earns five times the usual score for kills, but must be reloaded after every shot. The player with the highest score is the winner.

ESCALATION

In this Conflict style mode without loadouts, you must prove your abilities with a variety of weapons. Each kill moves you to the next weapon in a sequence. The first player to complete the full sequence and cap it with a rocket kill is declared the winner.

YOU ONLY LIVE TWICE

This mode is a variant of Conflict. You have a set number of lives that you can lose before you are removed from the game. The last player standing is the winner.

TEAM CONFLICT

Teamwork is the key to victory. Fight alongside your allies to kill enemies and earn points for your team. At the end of the match, the team with the highest total score is the winner.

DETONATOR AGENT

In this Conflict style mode players battle for ownership of a bomb counting down to detonation. As the time gets shorter, the kills increase in value. However, if the bomb isn't passed to another player with a melee strike before it detonates, be ready to pay a heavy price.

LOCAL SPLIT SCREEN AND PRIVATE MULTIPLAYER GAME MODIFIERS

Modifier	Description
Lives	Modify the number of lives players have in You Only Live Twice game mode.
Time Limit	How long the game will last.
Score Limit	Total score required to win.
Radar	Show or hide the GPS radar.
Radar Dots Always Visible	Player blips always display on the GPS radar when turned on, but behave normally if turned off.
Player Health	Adjust the amount of player health.
Sprint Duration	Adjust the duration for which players can sprint.
Weapon Damage	Adjust the weapon damage for all weapons.
Explosive Damage	Adjust the damage done by explosions.
Hot Shot Pro	Only shots to the head do damage, or head shots are ignored completely. Damage from explosions works normally.
Melee Only	No weapons or gadgets allowed—you can only attack enemies with your hands.
Singularity	Players explode when they come into contact with each other—this includes teammates if Friendly Fire is also enabled.
Move Your Feet	Players who do not move for more than three seconds are automatically killed and lose points.
Revenge	Players gain an increasing weapon damage boost each time they are killed. Making a kill resets the weapon damage to normal.
Rubber Grenades	All grenades become extremely bouncy.
Sticky Grenades	All grenades stick to players and any other surface on contact.
Nick Nack Mode	All players are shrunk to half their normal size and cannot vault or climb any obstacle.
Classic Health	Health no longer regenerates and Armor must be collected to protect yourself.
Friendly Fire	Friendly targets can be harmed.

GOLDEN GUN

This mode offers Conflict style gameplay with a special weapon to locate and use. The Golden Gun is a one-shot kill at any range and earns five times the usual score for kills, but must be reloaded after every shot. The player with the highest score is the winner.

CONFLICT

In Conflict there are no teams, no friends and only one rule: kill as many enemies as you can as fast as you can. The player with the highest score is the winner.

TEAM CONFLICT

Teamwork is the key to victory. Fight alongside your allies to kill enemies and earn points for your team. At the end of the match, the team with the highest total score is the winner.

BLACK BOX

MI6 must locate and destroy a crashed spy satellite black box recorder; the enemy team must retrieve and protect the box to download the data contained within. The team which completes its objective first is the winner.

GOLDENEYE

Teams capture and control consoles to move the GoldenEye satellite over their enemies' base. The team that holds the most consoles for the longest time wins.

HEROES

A player from each team is randomly chosen to be their Hero who is tougher, faster and deadlier. Heroes assist nearby teammates with temporary weapon and health enhancements, but are high-value targets for the enemy team. Heroes have infinite ammo and cannot swap weapons.

ESCALATION

In this Conflict style mode without loadouts, you must prove your abilities with a variety of weapons. Each kill moves you to the next weapon in a sequence. The first player to complete the full sequence and cap it with a rocket kill is declared the winner.

DETONATOR AGENT

In this Conflict style mode players battle for ownership of a bomb counting down to detonation. As the time gets shorter, the kills increase in value. However, if the bomb isn't passed to another player with a melee strike before it detonates, be ready to pay a heavy price.

DATA MINER

Be the first to download a data file in a single life, while preventing others from doing the same. Kill enemies to reset their progress, then take the smartphone they drop to accelerate your own download.

BOMB DEFUSE

Both teams are tasked with destroying each other's target, but there is only one bomb! The team who retrieves, plants and defends the bomb long enough for it to detonate is victorious, but only if they prevent the enemy team from defusing it and returning the favor.

LICENSE TO KILL

A variant of Conflict mode geared to experienced players. Weapon damage is significantly boosted and the HUD radar is disabled. Think you've got what it takes to make more kills than anyone else? This is the place to prove it.

TEAM LICENSE TO KILL

A variant of Team Conflict mode, this is a hardcore team game for experienced players with boosted weapon damage and HUD radar disabled. Stay alert and choose your targets wisely; friendly fire kills teammates just as quickly as enemies.

CLASSIC CONFLICT

This Conflict style mode allows you to play as your favorite Bond villain. Each has unique strengths and weaknesses to be exploited and some have their own signature weapons. Choose the character which best suits your play.

JAWS

Accurate with firearms and immune to falling damage, among other abilities Jaws receives less damage for headshots.

ODDJOB

Oddjob's abilities include rapid wound recovery and resistance to explosions. He can also throw his hat for one-shot kills.

BLOFELD

Blofeld's weapon skills grant him faster reloads, increased range and round capacity as well as enhanced frag grenades.

SCARAMANGA

Scaramanga can kill with a single shot from his Golden Gun. His abilities include enhanced weapon damage and accuracy.

DR. NO

Dr. No's bullet-proof cybernetic arms grant him benefits including enhanced weapon accuracy and reload speed.

BARON SAMEDI

Samedi's Voodoo arts grant him abilities such as enhanced health, resistance to bullet damage and rapid healing.

RED GRANT

Grant's abilities include longer sprint duration and increased health. He also carries the Red 96 fully automatic pistol.

ROSA KLEBB

Klebb uses the Pearl Grip 418 pistol and poison tipped Stiletto Blades, while KGB training enhances her weapon accuracy.

DR. KANANGA

Kananga has resistance to melee hits and enhanced weapon skills. He also carries the full-auto Compressed Air Pistol.

GOLDFINGER

Goldfinger has enhanced weapon damage, range and round capacity. He also uses a custom Gold Plated Revolver.

TEE HEE

Tee Hee's bullet-proof mechanical arm gives him enhanced weapon control and resistance to explosive damage.

MAX ZORIN

Zorin's abilities include rapid healing, increased health reserves, enhanced weapon accuracy and round capacity.

UNENHANCED MULTIPLAYER CHARACTERS

NATALYA

TREVELYAN

ONATOPP

OURUMOV

ZUKOVSKY

MISHKIN

HAZMAT

SOLDIER

PILOT

SECURITY

SKY BRIGGS

RED-ONE

RED-FOUR

RED-FIVE

RED-NINE

PVT. GUROV

PVT. KOZMIN

PVT. HARKOV

PVT. SHKADOV

JONES

DAVIS

SMYTH

ADAMS

TWO-TWO

TWO-FOUR

TWO-SIX

TWO-SEVEN

SGT. GLEBOV

SGT. BAIKOV

SGT. CHZOV

SGT. DRASHEV

FIVE-ONE

FIVE-TWO

FIVE-THREE

FIVE-FOUR

VINCENT

SLAV

**BORIS
RUSSIAN GUARD**

ALFONSO

SGT. MOROZOV

SGT. ZOTKIN

SGT. UDALOV

SGT. SHUBKIN

BOND

WEAPONS

Bond can carry two other weapons besides his P99. You cannot exchange the P99 for another weapon. All weapons have limited ammo, so conservation and a keen eye for dropped weapons is a must.

Each weapon has four stats: Damage, Accuracy, Range, and Rate of Fire. They are rated on a scale of 1-10 with 1 being the lowest rated and 10 being the highest.

PISTOLS

P99

STAT TYPE	STAT DETAIL
Damage	4
Accuracy	5
Range	3
Rate of Fire	4

Now the standard issue sidearm for all MI6 field agents, the P99 is compact and easily concealable—most commonly in an arm-pit rig or belt clip holster. With a standard clip size of 16 rounds and firing single shot semi-automatic, the P99 is a good all-around weapon but really shines when equipped with a silencer for silent kills on targets that are outside melee range.

TORKA T3

STAT TYPE	STAT DETAIL
Damage	5
Accuracy	4
Range	3
Rate of Fire	5

This Soviet era handgun may be uncomplicated compared to modern firearms, but this inherent simplicity is what makes it so easy to handle. With eight rounds in a standard magazine firing single shot semi-automatic, the Torka is an entry-level sidearm ideal for learning the basics of pistol combat.

HAWKSMAN M5A

STAT TYPE	STAT DETAIL
Damage	5
Accuracy	8
Range	4
Rate of Fire	4

A favored sidearm of black-ops teams, the Hawksman is renowned for its flexibility of purpose and can receive multiple attachments. While firing single shot semi-automatic, the standard clip capacity of 15 rounds is usually more than enough to drop a target at close range.

KUNARA V

STAT TYPE	STAT DETAIL
Damage	4
Accuracy	5
Range	3
Rate of Fire	8

The main purpose of the Kunara is simple: saturate the target with as much firepower as possible while still maintaining accuracy and effectiveness. The Kunara fires three-shot bursts with each trigger press, emptying a standard 21 round magazine in short order. The bursts are intended to ensure recoil is controlled well enough that subsequent bursts in quick succession are all on target.

WOLF .44

STAT TYPE	STAT DETAIL
Damage	8
Accuracy	4
Range	5
Rate of Fire	2

This nickel-plated revolver is the connoisseur's choice of sidearm. Lauded for the damage it can cause with a single bullet, its massive recoil is hard to tame. Having a standard revolver frame it only holds six rounds of ammunition, fired individually with each trigger pull. It's speed loader system ensures reloading is at least as fast as a magazine based weapon.

RED 96

STAT TYPE	STAT DETAIL
Damage	4
Accuracy	4
Range	3
Rate of Fire	8

A relic of two World Wars, this pistol was ahead of its time in firearm technology upon entering regular service in the early 1900's. This custom version holds ten rounds in a standard clip, capable of firing fully automatic. While it is almost a museum piece, it remains as effective as the day it was manufactured and intel suggests it is still the sidearm of choice for SPECTRE operatives.

COMPRESSED AIR PISTOL

STAT TYPE	STAT DETAIL
Damage	2
Accuracy	6
Range	3
Rate of Fire	10

This unique weapon was confiscated from Bond by Dr. Kananga on a previous mission and current intel suggests it may still be in Kananga's possession. Designed for use in air or underwater, it employs a compressed air system as the propulsion method rather than a traditional chemical explosion.

PEARL GRIP 418

STAT TYPE	STAT DETAIL
Damage	2
Accuracy	3
Range	2
Rate of Fire	5

This highly concealable and elegant pistol is favored by female SPECTRE agents working undercover as it can be secreted almost anywhere upon the body. With a standard clip size of seven rounds firing single shot semi-automatic, the 418 is a classy weapon. Don't be fooled by its tiny size—it is deadly in the right hands.

GOLD PLATED REVOLVER

STAT TYPE	STAT DETAIL
Damage	10
Accuracy	3
Range	4
Rate of Fire	2

This revolver has been modified and customized to suit the lavish tastes of its owner. With a flawless, precious metal plated finish, there is no doubt this weapon is almost worth its weight in gold. Chambering the standard six rounds for a revolver, it has a similar single shot, double-action mechanism to the Wolfe. The Gold Plated Revolver is intended to be admired for its looks as much as its combat effectiveness.

WEAPONS

SUBMACHINE GUNS

SIGMUS

STAT TYPE	STAT DETAIL
Damage	3
Accuracy	3
Range	3
Rate of Fire	7

Similar in shape and function to the Simgus 9, the smaller Sigmus SMG is still popular with tactical teams where mobility and rapid response to evolving mission parameters demand a lightweight automatic weapon. With a standard clip of 20 rounds firing fully automatic, the Sigmus can receive several tactical attachments, making it a good choice for short to medium range engagements.

SIGMUS 9

STAT TYPE	STAT DETAIL
Damage	4
Accuracy	4
Range	4
Rate of Fire	9

The Sigmus nine is a fully automatic weapon with the standard clip size of 30 rounds. It is the weapon of choice for armed police and Special Forces groups around the world due to its simplicity of operation and reliability. Its role in the field is highly flexible by virtue of receiving a large variety of tactical attachments.

STAUGER UA-1

STAT TYPE	STAT DETAIL
Damage	5
Accuracy	4
Range	5
Rate of Fire	8

The Stauger is one of the new breed of compact submachine guns specifically tailored to the demands of covert ops teams. The standard magazine holds an impressive 40 rounds and fires fully automatic. With a swing-down fore-grip and sliding shoulder stock, it can be fired from the hip for saturation/suppression fire, or from the shoulder for much more precise shot selection.

VARGEN FH-7

STAT TYPE	STAT DETAIL
Damage	3
Accuracy	2
Range	2
Rate of Fire	9

Every aspect of the Vargen has been refined by years of R&D to create the perfect submachine gun; from the lightweight but tough plastic frame to the tactical attachments it can receive. With a revolutionary horizontal mounted magazine and impressive 50 rounds of standard firing fully automatic, no other SMG can put as much firepower on the target in a short space of time.

STRATA SV-400

STAT TYPE	STAT DETAIL
Damage	5
Accuracy	6
Range	6
Rate of Fire	10

The Strata leads the field of next-generation compact weapons. Its main innovation is a system that re-vectors the effects of recoil in a downward direction rather than upward, almost completely negating barrel "rise," carrying 30 rounds in a standard magazine and capable of receiving numerous attachments on standard Picatinny rails, the Strata excels in short to medium range engagements.

ASSAULT RIFLES

AK-47

STAT TYPE	STAT DETAIL
Damage	4
Accuracy	3
Range	6
Rate of Fire	5

It is said that there are AK-47's in combat use today that were originally manufactured many decades previous, thanks to its legendary reliability. Not as tactically flexible as modern assault rifles, the standard 30 round magazine can be emptied rapidly with fully automatic fire, although the accuracy falls off sharply after the first few rounds. For best results short bursts of fire are recommended.

KALLOS-TT9

STAT TYPE	STAT DETAIL
Damage	5
Accuracy	4
Range	9
Rate of Fire	9

The Kallos has been tailored to suit current and potential future needs of special forces units. As a result, it can equip a wide variety of attachments and can be configured for a range of tactical situations. It retains the standard clip size of 30 rounds and fully automatic firing mode to match other assault rifles while exceeding the capabilities of many with its tactical flexibility.

TERRALITE III

STAT TYPE	STAT DETAIL
Damage	6
Accuracy	9
Range	7
Rate of Fire	8

The Terralite is an evolution of a rifle with over 50 years of field testing and refinement behind it. Carrying 30 rounds in a standard magazine, it fires three shot burst with each trigger pull. Standard issue for several military forces around the world, it has proven itself countless times as a multipurpose weapon, receiving a wide range of tactical attachments to suit any mission parameter.

ANOVA DP3

STAT TYPE	STAT DETAIL
Damage	5
Accuracy	6
Range	9
Rate of Fire	8

A favorite assault rifle of MI6 operatives, the Anova blends tactical flexibility with a lightweight frame for optimal combat effectiveness in the field. Firing fully automatic with a standard magazine capacity of 30 rounds, the Anova may lack the power of the Ivana but compensates for this with being able to receive a grenade launcher attachment for an explosive alternative fire mode.

IVANA SPEC-R

STAT TYPE	STAT DETAIL
Damage	7
Accuracy	8
Range	8
Rate of Fire	10

The Ivana is a Bullpup style rifle, which positions the standard 30 round magazine and firing mechanism behind the trigger, resulting in a compact and lightweight frame. The benefits are apparent when firing fully automatic; it is the most accurate rifle over medium long range. The only tangible downside is the lack of an appropriate grenade launcher attachment point.

WEAPONS

SNIPER RIFLES

PAVLOV ASR

STAT TYPE	STAT DETAIL
Damage	7
Accuracy	8
Range	9
Rate of Fire	2

This Russian-made sniper rifle is one of the most easily recognizable due to its long slender profile. While it is basic in design, like many Russian manufactured weapons, the reliability is enviable. Capable of firing semi-automatic it can unload a standard ten round magazine accurately at long range as long as the severe recoil is allowed to settle between shots.

AS15 MK12

STAT TYPE	STAT DETAIL
Damage	8
Accuracy	9
Range	10
Rate of Fire	2

This rifle is built around the basic Terralite frame but with modifications such as a longer barrel, weighted shoulder stock and high-powered optics. It is a weapon of power rather than precision. It holds ten rounds in a standard clip, firing semi-automatic. It sacrifices some stability for bullet power. It is tricky to use accurately at long range, but it's well worth the effort to master its idiosyncrasies.

28

TOROS AV-400

STAT TYPE	STAT DETAIL
Damage	8
Accuracy	9
Range	8
Rate of Fire	3

On the surface, the Toros seems a very average gun; holding only five rounds in a standard clip and firing semi-automatic. However it is only when using it in combat that its virtues become apparent due to its recoil stabilization functionality. It is capable of putting all five rounds in a very tight grouping at long range and in a short time. It is ideal for the sniper who likes to move position often.

WA2000

STAT TYPE	STAT DETAIL
Damage	8
Accuracy	9
Range	9
Rate of Fire	2

Don't be put off by the blocky and cumbersome looks of the WA2000. The shape is very carefully designed to enhance stability and accuracy, culminating in a perfectly balanced rifle. Holding six rounds in the standard clip and firing semi-automatic, the WA2000 is an elegant weapon with precision and power in equal proportions.

GAMBIT CP-208

STAT TYPE	STAT DETAIL
Damage	9
Accuracy	10
Range	9
Rate of Fire	1

The Gambit is one of the most powerful anti-personal sniper rifles in the world. It is only outmatched in power by much larger caliber anti-material rifles. Carrying only five rounds in a standard clip, this bolt-action rifle must be cycled after every shot, making it one of the slowest rifles to fire. However, when the power per shot is enough to kill a target at virtually any range, this negative aspect is easily overlooked.

SLY 2020

STAT TYPE	STAT DETAIL
Damage	9
Accuracy	2
Range	2
Rate of Fire	2

Often referred to as a "Sawn Off" shotgun due to its shortened barrel, the 2020 is simple in function, featuring a standard pump action. Lacking a formal shoulder stock, it is not as stable or accurate as other shotguns. While it must still be pumped after every shot to prime the next cartridge, the addition of a seven round removalable magazine removes the need to reload cartridges individually.

SEGS 550

STAT TYPE	STAT DETAIL
Damage	9
Accuracy	5
Range	3
Rate of Fire	3

Featuring traditional dimensions in terms of barrel length and shoulder stock, it is a step up in accuracy and effectiveness over the Sly 2020. While it holds eight rounds in the magazine tube it must be pumped after every shot to prime the next cartridge. It lacks the removeable magazine of the 2020 and therefore each cartridge must be reloaded individually by hand.

PT-9 INTERDICTUS

STAT TYPE	STAT DETAIL
Damage	8
Accuracy	5
Range	4
Rate of Fire	3

Designed specifically with military and special forces applications in mind, the Interdictus is a tactical shotgun and the only one capable of receiving a Reflex Site. Holding eight rounds in the magazine tube, it must still be pumped after every shot. It may be slow to reload but it's lightweight and ergonomic design help enhance its effectiveness, especially in a group or crowd situations.

DRUMHEAD TYPE-12

STAT TYPE	STAT DETAIL
Damage	6
Accuracy	3
Range	4
Rate of Fire	5

The Drumhead is an intimidating weapon for the shooter and target alike. The only shotgun capable of emptying its eight cartridge magazine tube with semi-automatic fire, it is outclassed in damage per second by the Masterton alone. The recoil is harsh when firing multiple shots in quick succession but the ability to unload the magazine tube quickly is a strong selling point.

MASTERTON M-557

STAT TYPE	STAT DETAIL
Damage	6
Accuracy	7
Range	5
Rate of Fire	8

While the Drumhead is a great firing semi-automatic, the Masterton takes the shotgun concept to the extreme with a fully automatic fire mode. The largest standard magazine capacity of all the shotguns, it holds 12 rounds which disappear quickly if the trigger is held in, but can be reloaded much faster than a standard shotgun.

WEAPONS

KL-033 MK2

STAT TYPE	STAT DETAIL
Damage	4
Accuracy	3
Range	3
Rate of Fire	8

On the border between submachine gun and the machine pistol, the KL-033 is a surprisingly effective weapon. The standard magazine holds 20 rounds and fires fully automatic. Historically it was renowned for being very inaccurate but this customized version addresses some of those issues. It still suffers from strong recoil, but fired in controlled bursts it is very efficient in short to medium range.

MJR 409

STAT TYPE	STAT DETAIL
Damage	10
Accuracy	9
Range	10
Rate of Fire	2

Traditionally an anti-vehicle weapon, this bulky launcher fires a single warhead at a time and is very slow to reload. Launching a high explosive rocket propelled grenade over long distances, the slow travel speed of the warhead is such that direct hits are virtually impossible. However the explosive splash damage is usually more than enough to kill an enemy if it detonates close enough.

MOONRAKER LASER

STAT TYPE	STAT DETAIL
Damage	5
Accuracy	7
Range	7
Rate of Fire	7

This high-tech laser-based weapon was designed to be used in space or in normal earth atmosphere and fires laser bolts with a fully automatic firing system. It features a recharging Power Cell allowing 40 uninterrupted shots to be fired, however the rate of a recharge is much slower than the rate of fire. Care must be taken to not drain the power cell before the target is eliminated.

PRIMARY WEAPON ATTACHMENTS

COMPENSATOR

Increases aiming accuracy when firing multiple successive shots. Weapon damage is slightly reduced when attached.

GRENADE LAUNCHER

Launches a fragmentation grenade over long distances via an additional firing mode. This attachment usually gives you three rounds of grenades and must be removed once empty in order to return to a normal mode of shooting.

ACOG SCOPE

A magnifying scope for better aiming. This is a mini-scope attachment for non-sniper rifle weapons. Perfect for long-range attacks.

LASER POINTER

Increases accuracy when shooting from the hip. A single laser beam is attached to the barrel of the gun and calibrated to point exactly where the bullet is headed.

THERMAL SCOPE

Highlights heat sources when aiming. Thermal Scopes are only available to weapons that already have a scope. All warm-blooded objects are animated through the scope as white glowing shapes to discern them from the non-biological background.

REFLEX SIGHT

Increases accuracy when using Iron Sights. A welcomed improvement over Iron Sight shooting.

WEAPONS

SECONDARY WEAPON ATTACHMENTS

SILENCER

Suppresses weapon noise and does not expose the player on the enemy radar when firing. Weapon damage is slightly reduced when attached.

COMPENSATOR

Increases aiming accuracy when firing multiple successive shots. Weapon damage is slightly reduced when attached.

LASER POINTER

Increases weapon accuracy. A single laser beam is attached to the barrel of the gun calibrated to point exactly where the bullet is headed.

GADGETS

These items are found in multiplayer modes. This is part of your loadout options before the game is initiated.

SMOKE SCREEN

Three smoke screen grenades that create a large cloud of smoke designed to mask movement.

FLASHBANG

Three flashbang grenades that generate an intensely bright flash with a secondary concussive-effect to stun targets.

TIMED MINE

Two high explosive sticky charges with a fixed duration fuse timer.

REMOTE TRIGGER MINE

Two high explosive sticky charges that are remotely detonated with your smartphone (press down on the D-pad).

PROXIMITY MINE

A single high explosive sticky charge with a proximity activated trigger. Best used to protect your flank when sniping.

FAST FORWARD

Increases overall movement speed. No increase when vaulting or climbing.

POLARIZED CONTACTS

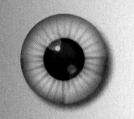

Neutralizes the blinding effect of flash grenades.

MINE SWEEPER

Detects nearby enemy mines and marks them on the HUD.

BIO BOOSTER

Increases your maximum health.

LAST CHANCE OF DEFIANCE

Drop a live frag grenade at your feet just after dying.

REACTIVE ARMOR

Reduces bullet and explosive damage received, giving you a fighting chance of surviving the detonation of a mine you didn't see.

SNAP SHOT

Improves your accuracy when firing from the hip.

SPEED LOADER

Cuts down the reload time on any firearm you are using.

HI-CAP MAGAZINE

Increased round capacity for your firearms.

HEAVY HITTER

Increased weapon damage. Enables hollow point ammo to cause maximum per round damage.

MULTITASK

Allows you to replace your secondary weapon (pistol) with an additional backup primary weapon.

WEAPONS

MISSION 1:
ARKHANGELSK

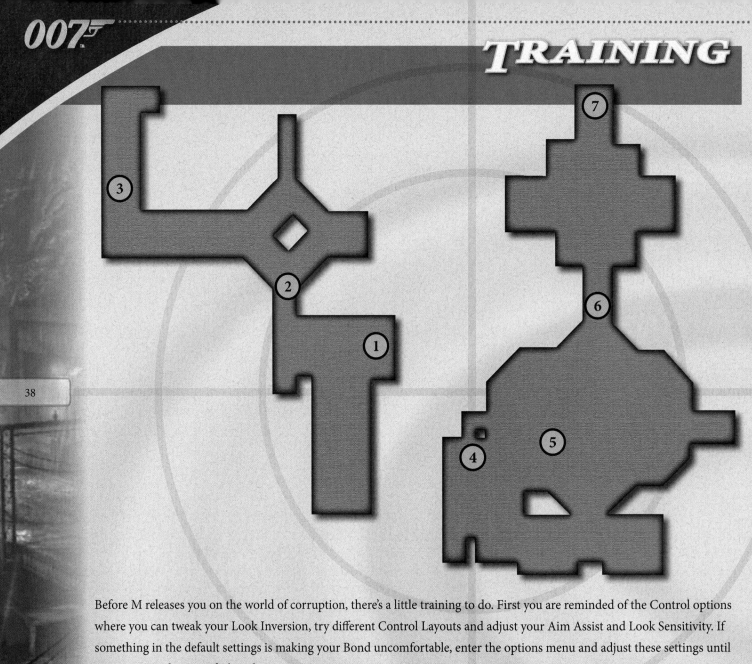

Before M releases you on the world of corruption, there's a little training to do. First you are reminded of the Control options where you can tweak your Look Inversion, try different Control Layouts and adjust your Aim Assist and Look Sensitivity. If something in the default settings is making your Bond uncomfortable, enter the options menu and adjust these settings until movement and aiming feels right.

GUN RANGE

PICK UP P99 FROM THE COUNTER

Head to the left counter beside the gun range stalls
(1). Once you are standing close enough, follow the onscreen
prompt to pick up the P99. You can hold up to three weapons
at a time. Take the weapon and reload it.

LOOK OUT AT THE FIRING RANGE

Look for the green "2" light above the firing lane which
indicates window 2. Take a stance at this shooting lane and
begin target practice. After the basic stuff, you learn how to
pop up from cover and auto-target as well as how to shoot an
enemy if *ADS Snap* is enabled in the options (which it is by
default).

PICK UP TWO ADDITIONAL WEAPONS

After some pop up targeting practice, walk back to the same counter and pick up two assault rifles from the available
assortment. You can take one of these death machines and lay waste to some lifeless targets or you can just wait a bit for your
next objective to be revealed.

USE THE RED BUTTON ON THE WALL.

Head toward the target marker and open the door by
approaching the switch and activating the indicated button
used for interacting with objects.

VAULTING

Once through the doorway you are confronted with a hallway barrier (2) that begs you to show off your vaulting skills. Once over the barrier you follow the objective marker to a stairway. In this stairway you are instructed on the use of a silencer with the P99.

SPRINTING

After vaulting over the hallway barrier you are introduced to the sprint control. Sprinting only lasts for a short period of time, but there's next to zero recovery time. Just punch the button again and hold it to get the quickest run out of James.

SILENCER

Press left on the D-Pad to screw on the silencer. Using silenced weapons keeps you in stealth until a living guard sees a neighboring guard shot dead—silently. You can prevent an enemy alert by quickly killing any witnesses. The P99 is really the best weapon for this. From any distance, most unarmored guards cannot live after four or five shots. A headshot brings instantaneous death.

GO TO THE BASEMENT
USING VENTS

Always be on the lookout for ventilation shafts (4). Vents are usually alternate routes that lead to locations behind enemy lines or are sometimes the only way to get beyond a locked door. Remove the cover using the interact button and crawl through the vent until you find an exit—or multiple exits. You often discover a stealth kill opportunity at the end of a ventilation pathway.

STEALTH KILL: SILENTLY SUBDUE ENEMIES

When you scuttle to the end of the ventilation shaft, unhinge the cover and creep through a cubicle pathway. In the following office you are presented with an option to stealthily dispose of those unsuspecting enemies. Put the chokehold of death on the soldier (5) in this room by pressing the right control stick button down.

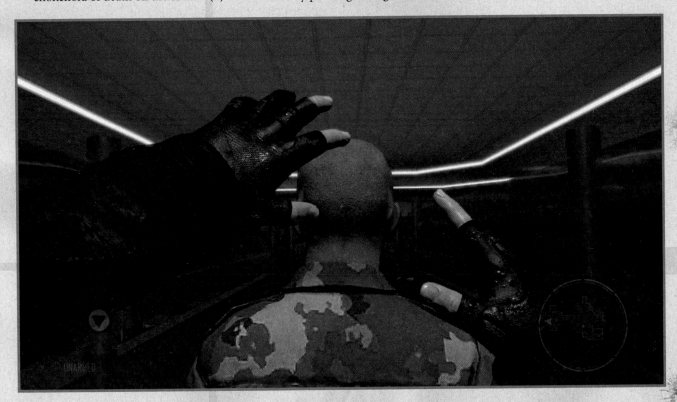

SECURITY CAMERAS

After silently dispatching the guard, you come to a hallway (6) where a tip prompt pauses gameplay. If you had walked any further without shooting the security camera at the end of the hallway you would have failed the mission. Taking out security cameras before they spot you keeps the enemy from reinforcing the area.

DISPATCH THE GUARD

Your last challenge in training is to shoot the soldier on the elevator (7) when the doors open. Go ahead and lock your aim on him and fire off a handful of rounds in quick succession so he has no chance to call for help or to fire his weapon. Enter the elevator and press the control panel to end the training session.

DAM

NORTHERN DVINA RIVER • ARKHANGLESK OBLAST, RUSSIAN FEDERATION

PRIMARY OBJECTIVES

Infiltrate the Dam

Secure Transport

Gather Intel on the EMP Hardened Helicopter

SECONDARY OBJECTIVES

Erase the Security Footage (2)

Download the Flight Plan

Before the first mission begins, MI6 briefs you on the job. For the past three years, Arkady Ourumov, a high-ranking Russian general, has been stealing Russian military equipment and selling it on the black market. M's afraid the latest shipment is finding its way into the hands of terrorists that have been targeting English embassies. Along with agent 006, you must infiltrate his base of operations, destroy the weapons cache, and if need be, eliminate the general.

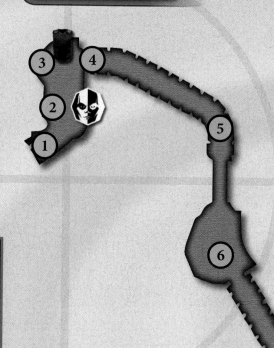

INFILTRATE THE DAM

You meet 006 (1) perched high on a dark and rainy mountainside, overlooking a Russian outpost. The two of you slide down the mountain slope and come up behind two guards with their backs to you. 006 takes out the guy on the left while you subdue the one on the right. With that done, 006 moves across the road and waits for you to start the gun battle with the many guards around the tower (3).

Head through the ditch (2) and climb out on the other side. Crouch down and take cover behind the cement barricade. These barricades crumble under gunfire so be aware that you may need to reposition yourself while the shootout occurs or even find entirely new cover, depending on how it goes.

JANUS SYMBOL #1

Enter the conduit in the ditch that passes under the road. Find and shoot the Janus symbol located on the top of this large sewage pipe near a large hole. There are 50 Janus Symbols in all and four or five in each mission, so keep your eyes peeled.

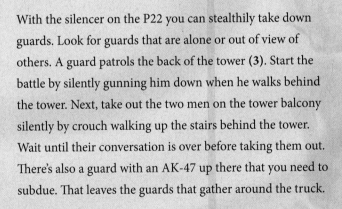

With the silencer on the P22 you can stealthily take down guards. Look for guards that are alone or out of view of others. A guard patrols the back of the tower (3). Start the battle by silently gunning him down when he walks behind the tower. Next, take out the two men on the tower balcony silently by crouch walking up the stairs behind the tower. Wait until their conversation is over before taking them out. There's also a guard with an AK-47 up there that you need to subdue. That leaves the guards that gather around the truck.

If you don't feel like subduing, take out the sniper on the tower next, as he's the most threatening target. Then work on dropping the guards around the truck (4), which begin to scatter when you drop the sniper. Normally, you would want to blow up the truck by shooting the gas tank below the door to take out all the enemies standing nearby, but you need this vehicle. For that reason it does not explode.

Make sure to put four or five rounds into an enemy in quick succession to drop them before they can warn anyone or call for backup. A headshot is more difficult but it takes an enemy out with one squeeze of the trigger.

With all the red blipped enemies off your radar, rush into the top floor of the sniper tower **(3)** using the interior or exterior stairs. Inside the tower control room you find two **Pavlov ASR + Multiple Attachments**. Take one. Reload and then take the other. Find **Armor** on the table next to a rifle. Enemies now enter the area where you started **(1)**.

Using the sniper rifle, shoot these new arrivals through the tower doorway. The sniper rifle is so powerful that you can actually pass a single bullet through two aligned enemies! Once you've eliminated these four new targets, enter the truck **(4)** through the passenger door. 006 takes the driver's seat.

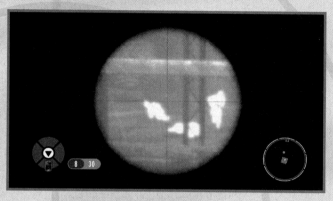

SECURE TRANSPORT AND INFILTRATE THE DAM

While 006 drives he reveals a little intel on the target. Everything goes swimmingly until you reach the first checkpoint at the end of the tunnel **(5)**. Two guards try to evict you from the truck, but 006 quickly guns them both down and you grab the **AK** from the hands of the falling guard on your side of the truck. Use this weapon to eliminate threats as 006 tries to speed to safety.

RIDING SHOTGUN

You're armed with an AK47 and 006 has the wheel. All you need to concentrate on is shooting the biggest threats to your life as you travel along the top of the dam, passing through multiple tunnels full of armed soldiers and clearings with armed vehicles. Reload in the lulls of the battle and always be on the lookout for the biggest threat. The most damaging attacks come from the gunmen shooting from the back of military trucks **(6)** that drive in front of you. Target these gunmen before any other target options.

After surviving the first tunnel, you come to a clearing (7). Blast the walking soldiers from behind, reload and begin targeting the machine-gunner on top of the jeep that speeds past you on the right. Try to take him out before you enter the next tunnel where more truck gunmen attack. At the entrance (8) to the next tunnel you must press the button displayed at the bottom of the screen to hit a clingy soldier with the butt of your rifle. This causes him to swing out on your door and takes care of that immediate problem.

A horizontally parked fuel truck blocks the entrance to the next tunnel (9). Shoot the tank to blow up the truck, allowing 006 to pass. In the next clearing (10) an unavoidable event occurs. Two RPGs are launched from a nearby guard tower. The first one is enough to make 006 jump from the truck and Bond soon follows.

During this cinematic, James spots a large attack helicopter landing on a nearby helipad. 006 pries open the doors to an elevator shaft and the two of you slide down to a lower level entrance to the interior dam facility.

GATHER INTEL ON THE EMP HARDENED HELICOPTER

DAM INTERIOR F2

When you reach the bottom of the elevator shaft, 006 waits for your move to infiltrate the room **(11)** beyond the elevator doors. Press the indicated button to breach the room.

If you are not fast enough, the enemies in the breach hit an alarm on the left wall, alerting enemies in the area. You see the rightmost guard make a b-line for this switch when the challenge begins. Take him out first. Gun down the three men inside the control room during a slow-motion shooting challenge. 006 covers the elevator shafts and wants you to press on and not worry about taking a picture of the attack helicopter. Find the **Armor** in the room on a counter near the window.

An on screen tip reminds you that the smartphone icon flashes on screen when you are near an objective that requires the use of the smartphone.

SECONDARY MISSION OBJECTIVE: ERASE THE SECURITY FOOTAGE (1/2)

Shoot the padlock off the back door in this first room to uncover a server room. Pull out the smartphone and aim it at the node on the back wall. Press and hold the indicated button to hack the node. Your target indicator must be green before you can hack. This means you are within hacking range.

JANUS SYMBOL #2

The moment you leave the control room you can find a Janus Symbol by turning around and facing the doorway. Look behind the right door to find the Janus high up on the wall. Shoot it.

Enter the connecting hallway and peer over the right railing to the lower level **(F1)**. You see a troop transport truck pull up. Try to shoot the gas tank under the passenger's side door using a rifle (the Pavlov sniper rifle is a good choice here). Blow it up using any weapon to take out multiple enemies at once. Before concerning yourself with survivors and reinforcements, target and shoot the soldier coming up the stairs **(12)**. If the enemy didn't manage to set off the alarm in the previous challenge, you can move stealthily in this area, taking out patrolling and idling guards. However, if you alert these enemies, backup enemies spawn.

46

Look back over the railing and take out the enemies near the large, closed doorway below (13). You have the height advantage and it feels as easy as shooting fish in a barrel. Once the area is clear, head down to the lower floor.

DAM INTERIOR F1

At the large closed door (13) on floor 1, you can find a padlocked door to the left near the barricade. Next to the large closed door is an operational door switch. You have a choice of either attacking the next squad through this doorway or following a lower tunnel (14) to the balcony (15) in the next section. If you managed to get this far without raising an alarm, then take the maintenance hatch route to continue stealthily. If not, we suggest using the door, as the balcony leaves you open to too many enemy attack angles.

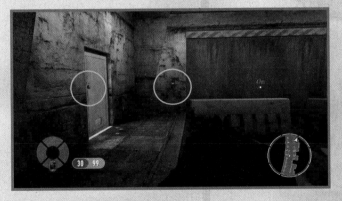

Clear the enemies from the next section (15) and make sure to get the one on the high right balcony before he takes you out. Once it's clear, enter the lower right entry, following the blip on the radar. Enter the docks through the closed double doors (16).

THE PIERS

Move quickly to the set of crates just before the piers. Target the red fuel barrel and shoot it just as the soldiers gather around the boat. You can also target the boat engines for an explosion. The second boat unloads its guards on the next pier. Gun them down before they get to cover.

JANUS SYMBOL #3

When you walk out onto the first pier **(17)** to check out the weapon crate at the end, you can spot the third Janus symbol on your way back. It is located high on the dam wall adjacent to the pier. Shoot it.

Find a silenced **Sigmus** in a weapon crate at the end of the first pier **(17)**. Shoot the lock off the case to pop it open. This is a good weapon to have now. The silencer helps keep you stealthy and many enemies carry a Sigmus, making ammo plentiful.

Shoot the padlock from the gate **(18)** beyond the piers. In this recessed alley you can find a closed door on the left, as well as a small ventilation shaft **(19)** just before the door near the bottom of the stairs.

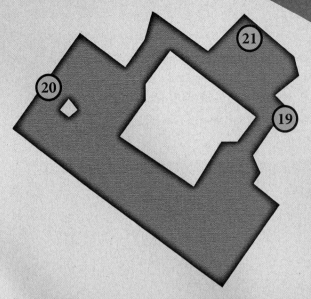

PUMP ROOM

We suggest using the ventilation shaft (19) to enter the pump room. If you go through the door you alert the nearby guard on the balcony overlooking the pump room. Going through the vent allows you to hit him with some silenced rounds or you can silently subdue him.

Look down the stairs and silently shoot the two guards on the metal catwalk. There's a security camera in the back left corner of this pump room and one in the glassed in office on the far right (20). We suggest remaining around the entry stairs and using the sniper rifle to shatter the glass in the distant control room and then start sniping all the soldiers inside. A couple of backup soldiers arrive via the next elevator (21), but they are far away and you have plenty of shot choices to get rid of them without much risk.

After clearing all the enemies in the area, enter the control room (20) just to pass through to the balcony on the original side of the room. Take the elevator (21) back up to the first dam level.

As the elevator doors open at the base of the helipad (22) you spot three patrolling guards. Silently shoot the closest one on the catwalk while remaining in the lift. Then shoot the two distant guards near the highest set of catwalk stairs you can see. Do this in quick succession and you can remain stealthy all the way to the top to the helipad.

Remain in the elevator. Wait for two more guards to run down the distant stairs into view and then shoot them. This only happens if you blow your cover. Begin climbing the catwalk stairs while facing the direction of the remaining guards so you can gun them down as soon as a shot opportunity arises.

At the top of the stairs you come to the upper dam level where you find a locked gate and a weapon crate. Take the **Pavlov ASR + Thermal Scope**. Head up the remaining stairs to reach the top of the helipad (23) where the EMP Hardened Helicopter is located.

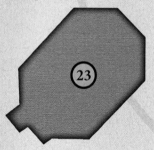

HELIPAD
GATHERING INTEL ON THE EMP HARDENED HELICOPTER

Stand and face the front of the helicopter (23). Select your smartphone and aim it at the helicopter's nose. Move closer or further to get a green go light for a focused shot on the weapon on the front of the airship.

You need two more shots. While facing the front of the helicopter, strafe left and right to get pictures of the Gatling gun on the left and the missile launcher on the right. That fulfills the current objective.

Two guards appear at the gate below, near the weapon case. Quickly gun them down and then shoot the gas tank of the troop transport vehicle that is screeching to a halt on the dam. This takes out all the occupants.

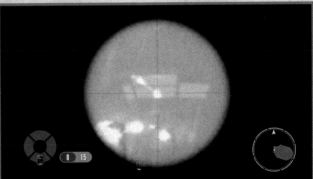

When you've eliminated all the advancing guards from the dam, place your sights on the distant guard tower (24). From the helipad you can snipe the sniper before he snipes you.

JANUS SYMBOL #4
Before heading for the sniper tower (24), head south on the dam to the south guard tower (25). Climb the stairs and, before you enter the tower, look around the left edge to find a ledge containing the fourth Janus symbol.

WALKTHROUGH

TOP OF THE DAM
SOUTH GUARD TOWER

While at the tower **(25)** for the Janus symbol, get your hands on the **MJR-409** rocket launcher inside. You can easily take out groups of guards by targeting vehicles near the enemy on the top of the dam. If you'd rather have an **AK**, you can find one in a chest near the surface-to-air gun across from the south tower.

Make your way cautiously to the north tower **(24)**. Expect a couple of attack waves as you get nearer. Use the columns for cover and try targeting vehicles to make them explode near the troops. The sniper rifle allows you to pick off all the enemies from a distance before they reach their appropriate firing distance. One soldier—in a group of three enemies in an attack wave—originates from inside the north tower. Watch the stairwell through the scope and be ready to fire.

SECONDARY MISSION OBJECTIVE: DOWNLOAD THE FLIGHT PLAN

When you've eliminated all the enemies, enter the north tower **(24)** and use your smartphone to hack the wi-fi node on the short wall near the stairs, just under the lookout window. This completes this extra objective.

Before you download the flight plan, two groups of four guards move in from the south dam. You can easily eliminate these groups of guards by aiming through the lookout window with the sniper rifle. If you let them get too close, some climb the stairs and come up behind you shooting. So keep an eye on your radar. Enter the elevator at the base of the north tower. Use the switch inside to reenter the dam facility.

DAM INTERIOR F2

SECONDARY MISSION OBJECTIVE: ERASE THE SECURITY FOOTAGE (2/2)

When you reach the dam interior again **(26)**, notice the room to your left that you can see through a bulletproof window. There is a security footage node on the wall near a door. Use a silenced weapon to shoot through the small square hole in the bullet proof window while targeting the lock on the door. You can now enter that room when you reach it in a little while. A guard is in the next room, so do this quietly or take him out first. You can subdue or silently shoot this guard.

From the window of the adjacent room, target and shoot the waves of soldiers below. You can take them all out rather easily from your high position. Try exploding the truck to take out enemies near it.

Enter the open doorway to the right **(27)** and climb down the ladder to the lower level.

DAM INTERIOR F1

Make your way to the left side of the new area and climb the stairs **(28)** up to the next level. Pivot around at the top of the stairs and you find the room **(29)** that you opened by shooting the door lock through the bulletproof glass. Once inside the small room, turn back towards the door and use your smartphone to hack the node to complete the extra objective.

Return downstairs and enter the section through the double doors **(29)**. Head up the set of stairs to reach dam level F2 again. Look over the right railing and you find 006 near a Humvee. Approach him to complete the mission.

In a cutscene, 006 escapes the encroaching troops by leaping off the side of the dam with a parachute. Bond is caught before he can jump. The soldiers ask for his chute and 007 complies. Just before handing it over he pulls the ripcord and leaps off the side of the dam, protected by the swelling parachute.

WALKTHROUGH

PRIMARY OBJECTIVES

Infiltrate the Weapons Facility

Release the Lockdown

Rendezvous with Agent 006

Sabotage the Fuel Tanks

Rendezvous with Agent 006

SECONDARY OBJECTIVES

Gather Intel for MI6 Analysis (3)

Download the Trade Manifests

INFILTRATE THE WEAPONS FACILITY

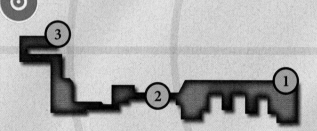

Having leapt off the Arkangelsk Dam, Bond enters the Chemical Facility hidden in the bowels of the dam to rendezvous with his contact, 006. After meeting Trevelyan (1), Bond gives him a hand to reach an upper catwalk. You meet up with him later. For now, enter the ventilation shaft (2).

Follow the ventilation route to the end and you come to a dead-end where two open vents point down into a bathroom below (3). You can get a clear shot of the enemy's head through the first vent. If you approach the second opening you can choose to drop down and silently subdue the guard on the toilet. When prompted, press the indicated button to successfully perform a stealth kill. This unlocks the "Royal Flush" Achievement or Trophy.

While crawling down to attack the guard you may have noticed the **AK** resting on the toilet in the adjacent stall. Open that door and take the weapon before you leave the room.

EXITING THE BATHROOM

If you allow the bathroom door (4) to slide open and face the hallway without entering the hallway, then the enemies in the next section do not become active yet. You can shoot out the glass in the hallway wall dead ahead of you without causing an alert. Do this and then step out into the hallway. Wait until you see a guard (5) pass beyond the glass. Shoot the guard with your silenced P99.

MACHINE ROOM

To enter the machine room (8) you can either go through the door at the end of the hallway (6) or you can head down to the lower passage where you dispatched the guard (5) through the glass and enter through a lower door (7). Either way you face the same amount of resistance. If you don't contain enemy movement through the room you have to watch your back, as the enemy works their way through the connecting passages to come up behind you.

The machine room is full of enemies so keep an eye on your radar for possible ambushes. These guards throw grenades, so be prepared to gun them down before they throw or clear out of the area if they lob one at you. Once the machine room is clear, follow the objective marker and use the exit (9) on the first floor to reach the offices.

RELEASE THE LOCKDOWN

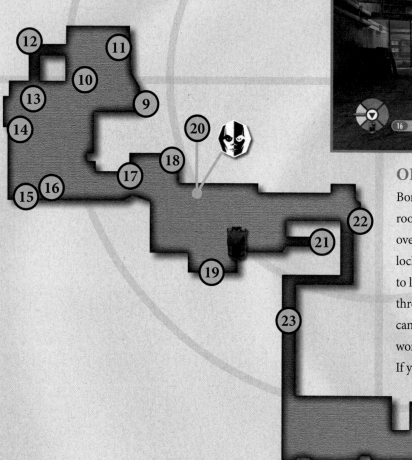

OFFICES

Bond enters the offices through the machine room doorway (9) and is informed by Trevelyan over radio communications that he has triggered a lockdown. Ourumov begins commanding soldiers to look for the intruders. You must now sneak through a series of offices, avoiding the security cameras and stealthily dispatching any facility workers and soldiers you come into contact with. If you alert anyone, a firefight ensues.

On the radar you can see multiple workers and a guard in the office area. The best way to move through this area is by crouching and entering the first office on the right (10). Continue crouching and creeping toward the man sitting at the desk (11). Silently subdue him. Shoot the padlock off the weapon locker in the same office and take the **Sigmus 9's**, if so desired.

Find the ventilation duct **(12)** on the upper level in this room. Follow this shaft to the next office **(13)**.

In the second office, first silently shoot the guard **(14)** near the stairs to the hallway and then shoot the distant worker at his desk in the next office **(15)**. Next, shoot the security camera in the hallway near the downed soldier **(14)**. If you alert reinforcements they come through the next doorway **(16)** in the far office.

Now exit the first set of offices through the next doorway **(16)**. Shoot the padlock off the door **(17)** at the end of the next hallway to enter a utility closet. Use the ventilation shaft in the closet to reach the next office area. You spot two guards walking away from you down an L-shaped corridor. After they pass out of sight, shoot the security camera **(18)** near the ceiling in the corner above the crates.

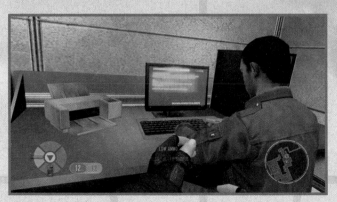

Creep around the corner the guards passed by and silently shoot the guard at the vending machine **(19)**. Continue crouch walking and enter the office on the left and silently subdue the guard **(20)** at the computer.

JANUS SYMBOL #5

While in the office (20), look behind a cabinet on the left side of the room to find this Janus symbol. Shoot it with a silenced weapon to keep moving stealthily through the offices.

SECONDARY MISSION OBJECTIVE: GATHER INTEL FOR MI6 ANALYSIS (1/3)

Before you leave the office area, enter the last office and take a picture of the blueprints on the back wall. This is the first of three pictures you need to take to complete this secondary mission.

Enter the next stairwell through doorway at the end of the hall. In this area you can find two passageways to the Cavity. Head down the stairs and find the **Armor** in the small, gated area in the corner. Under the same stairs you find a weapon locker. Shoot the padlock off and find two **Sigmus 9's with Silencers**. This is a good weapon to use in the next area. If you pass through the next doorway **(21)** on this lower level you enter a short hallway and through the next door you can reach the Cavity on its main level. However, this is not the best way to go.

Instead, head back up the stairs. Near the doorway you originally came through you spot a side hallway. Enter this area and look for the vent **(22)** near the floor. Use this ventilation shaft to enter the Cavity **(23)**.

CAVITY

Bond enters the Cavity area to the sound of security alarms and soldiers running to find the source of the intrusion alert that Trevelyan triggered.

Entering the Cavity through the high ventilation shaft **(22)** allows you to easily pick off all the guards on the lower level while remaining hidden. Even if your cover is blown, the large pipes you crouch along offer a lot of protection, however, you cannot return to the ventilation shaft for protection. You also have the height advantage on the enemy. Eliminate all the guards in the Cavity before moving down to their level. There is one guard that may be difficult to shoot. This guard is in the office straight across from your vent entry point. Unfortunately, this office is protected with bulletproof glass. If he reveals himself at the open doorway then take him out, otherwise you must wait until enter that room to dispatch him.

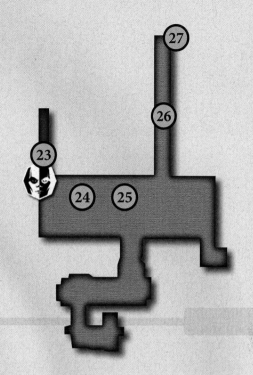

If things get really bad, it's best to proceed quickly along the scaffold to reach the office rooftops ahead. Follow the pipes from the vent to a high catwalk. Follow the catwalk a little ways and look through the right railing to spot a Janus symbol.

JANUS SYMBOL #6
When you enter the Cavity through the high ventilation shaft look to the right as you cross the high catwalk to spot this Janus Symbol above an office window. **(23).**

Head to the end of the high catwalk to access the rooftop of one of two offices on this side of the Cavity. Both office rooftops have a ceiling access hole. Do not enter the first one **(24)** or you miss the opportunity to progress the secondary mission: *Downloading the Trade Manifests.*

60

SECONDARY MISSION OBJECTIVE: DOWNLOADING THE TRADE MANIFESTS.

Enter the second ceiling access point (25) after entering the Cavity through the ventilation shaft (22). Drop into the room and find the green node on the wall in a corner. Use your smartphone to download the sensitive data.

Shoot the security camera in the next room and head down the stairs, eliminating any new guards that have shown up. Follow the objective marker across the catwalk bridge and through the next corridor doorway **(26).**

In the hallway are a ventilation shaft **(27)** and an unlocked door, each allowing access into the next office area. Take the ventilation shaft so you can move through the new office area killing stealthily, instead of initiating a chaotic shootout.

Once through the vent, find and use the next vent access in the area between the walls.

OFFICES

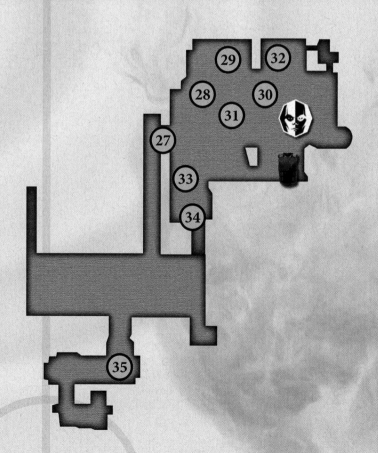

Once you've gained access to the first office through the ventilation shaft, silently subdue the guard at the computer in the corner **(28)**.

Use the untraveled ventilation shaft connected to this room to reach the next office **(29)**. There are no enemies in this office. Slowly look out the next doorway and notice the enemy sitting with his back toward you in a cubicle to the left. In the left corner just outside of the office is a security camera. Silently shoot the camera and then subdue the sitting enemy **(30)**.

Now move across the cubicle area while remaining crouched and subdue the guard working in a standing position on a console **(31)**. If you have not set off an alert, then all is good and only one more target remains in the office area. Follow the blip on the radar to this remaining guard **(32)**.

Enter the office on the opposite side of the room while remaining crouched and silently subdue the sitting guard at the desk **(32)**.

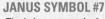

JANUS SYMBOL #7
Find the seventh Janus symbol on the inside corner wall of a small cubicle that houses some servers on the first floor of the second office area.

Before leaving the office area, check out the office near the exit hallway. Inside is a locked weapon chest. Shoot it open and decide if you need the **Sigmus 9 with the Reflex Sight**. In the server room above this office you can find an **Armor** power-up if you are playing 007 Classic mode.

Use the stairs in the office to reach the second level and access a short hallway with a small set of stairs leading to an unlocked door **(33).** This door allows you access back to the Cavity area.

MASTER ENGINEER'S OFFICE

Upon breaching the door **(33)** and entering the enemy-occupied office, slow-motion mode is engaged and you are challenged to gun down the two gunmen, leaving the lead engineer unscathed. With that done, approach the engineer and Bond automatically grabs him and begins to extract info. Press the indicated buttons to get the engineer's full cooperation. Afterward, you subdue the man if you press the correct indicated button. The master engineer removes the lockdown so you can enter the atrium area of the facility.

RENDEZVOUS WITH AGENT 006
CAVITY AREA REVISITED

Before you leave the room, check out the weapon crate in the corner and take the **AS 15 MK 12 with Silencer** from inside. When you exit the room through the open doorway you find yourself on a new balcony (**34**) back in the Cavity area.

From this bird's eye view of the Atrium, you can silently snipe each guard walking around on the different levels of catwalks. Target the enemy when they're alone so you don't trigger any alerts. Once all the enemies are gone, vault over the rail to land on the catwalk path below. Follow the objective marker to the now unlocked door (**35**), which is on the opposite side of the cavity.

ATRIUM

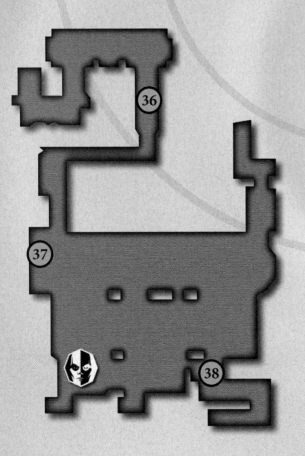

Follow the hallway to the end and enter the Atrium. You enter this new area on the highest level of the catwalks (**36**). Just around the corner you run into Agent 006. Trevelyan covers Bond using a silenced sniper rifle and helps you take down several guards. Begin by targeting the three guards that enter the lower level through an entry to your right (**37**). Take out the guards as they begin to separate to their assigned patrol positions. That way they don't see the others drop.

If you silently take out these three, then there are only two more enemies on the opposite side of the room and on different levels—that is if you did not raise an alert. Head down the stairs and look for one more guard to appear. Take him out and then look along the right wall to locate a Janus symbol.

JANUS SYMBOL #8
Find this Janus in a small crevice between a wall in the Atrium and one of its large tanks on the bottom floor.

There are two exits out of the Atrium **(38)** & **(39)**. One **(39)** leads to the continuing main objective while the other **(38)** leads to a secondary objective.

SECONDARY MISSION OBJECTIVE: GATHER INTEL FOR MI6 ANALYSIS (2/3)

The second intel gathering object is located through the secondary door **(38)** in the Atrium. Follow the hallway up to a room on the second floor. Dispatch the two guards and disable the security camera. Take a photo of the blueprints on the wall in the back office.

If you enter the upstairs office to gather intel, then also raid the weapon locker up there for the **Anova DP3 + ACOG Scope**. Then leave the Atrium through the previous door **(38)**. This is an airlock and the next doorway dumps you into the labs.

CLEAN LABS

Once through the airlock (**39**) you enter the Clean Labs area. There's a security camera (**40**) in the hallway dead ahead and you can also spot patrolling guards. This is a small area and there's no real reason to worry about stealth here. If you shoot the security camera first, the noise alerts the soldiers in the area. Use the airlock doorjambs for cover and just start mowing down enemies with an assault rifle. If the enemies toss a grenade, find new cover. There's a very small vent below the security camera that allows you to do nothing more than cut that corner of the hallway.

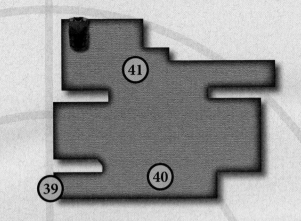

SECONDARY MISSION OBJECTIVE: GATHER INTEL FOR MI6 ANALYSIS (3/3)

After wasting all the enemies in the Clean Lab hallways, activate the computer in the corner (**41**) to unlock the door beside the computer. Enter the room and take a picture of the blueprint on the wall. Find **Armor** and **Anova DP3's with ACOG Scopes** in the corner weapon locker.

PRODUCTION LABS

Exit the Clean Labs by heading down the small set of stairs and passing through the unlocked door (**42**). In the Production Labs, enter the central area (**43**) following the arrow on the radar. Through an observation window on the left you see 006 enter the Production Lab through a vent.

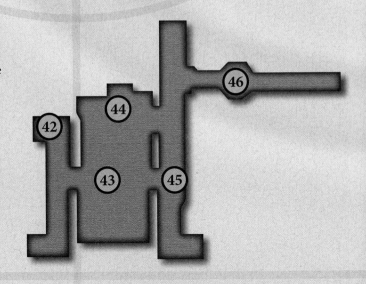

The lab has three scientists inside. He needs you to create a diversion so he isn't spotted. Use your smartphone to hack the node (44) above the doorway in 006's lab. You have to get right up against the observation window to get in range. This sets off an alarm. Most scientists escape the room before the door seals. 006 takes out the remaining man and then starts hacking computers.

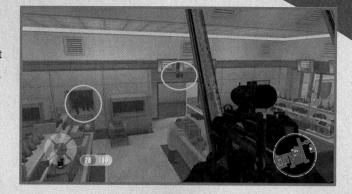

Enter the next hallway (45) and wait for 006 to hack the next few doors so you can get to the Fuel Tanks. Enter the next airlock chamber (46).

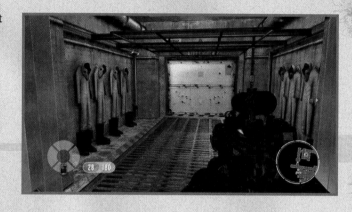

FUEL TANKS

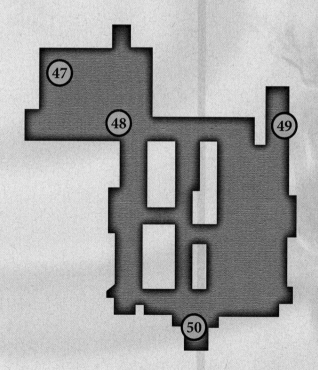

Bond leaves Trevelyan in order to set the explosives on the fuel storage tanks. In the first hallway you come up behind a patrolling guard. Silently shoot him in the back and continue to the hallway with an observation window. You can watch 006 attack two guards and then hack the door locks. This allows you access through the door (47) to your right.

Once in the same room with 006, enter the fuel containment room through the doorway **(48)** to his right. The first thing you spot is a security camera on the far side of the room **(49)**. Silently shoot it and any guards you can see on the lower level. Shoot through gaps in the tanks to take out another security camera **(50)** at the front of the room. While aiming in that area, eliminate the guard below this camera as well.

This part often turns into a large, *un-stealthy* gun battle, so have your assault rifle loaded and ready to go. You have the upper hand in the battle for the most part because of your height advantage and being able to retreat back into the previous room for cover. However, if you don't keep your eyes on the radar, many soldiers quickly come for you. It's best to remain stealthy as long as possible to get in those first few kills to lessen their numbers.

Once you eliminate all the enemies in the room you can now concentrate on placing one explosive on each of the six tanks in the room. Attach the explosives to the highlighted areas on the tanks. Each tank without an explosive attached is marked on the radar. Keep an eye on it if you need help keeping track of which tanks you've already placed bombs on. There are multiple locations on each tank where you can stick the explosives (accessible from both levels of the room). You only need one explosive per tank. Once you've set all six, leave the room through the next doorway **(50)**.

Bond finishes placing the explosives and makes his way to rendezvous with Trevelyan. While walking through the connecting hallway, Bond continually calls 006 but he oddly never responds. Enter the bottling room through the next door **(50)**.

BOTTLING ROOM

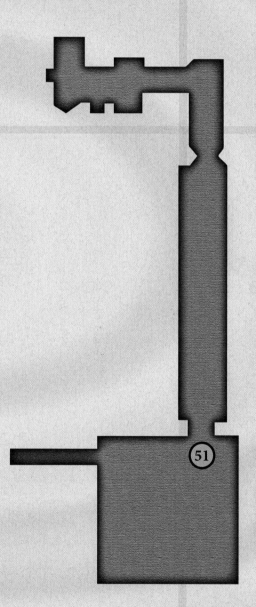

Bond walks straight into a room where Trevelyan is being held at gunpoint by Ourumov **(51)** and several guards. While Bond takes cover behind a rolling missile cart he is tricked into dropping his weapon and then witnesses Trevelyan's execution. As Ourumov approaches you, press the indicated button to set off the explosives. The blast causes chaos in the room, allowing Bond to escape up a conveyor belt.

WALKTHROUGH

PRIMARY OBJECTIVES

Escape from the Facility

SECONDARY OBJECTIVES

Neutralize the Helicopter Gunship

Destroy the Air Tracking Consoles

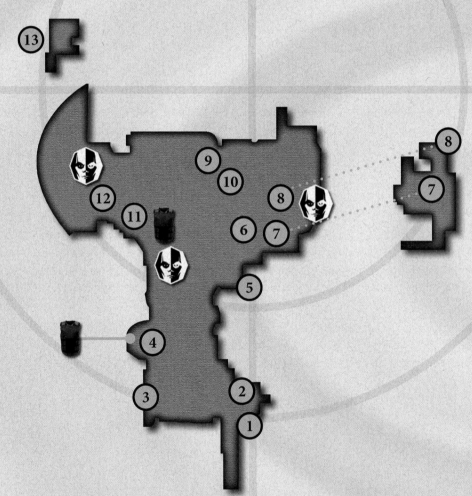

ESCAPE FROM THE FACILITY

Having detonated his limpet mines in the Chemical Facility, Bond escapes the degrading base and finds himself outside the facility close to a military airstrip. On the runway, a light aircraft is preparing for take-off. Bond must fight his way to the plane, his only means of escape from the impending destruction of Arkangelsk.

ATTACK HELICOPTER

As you enter the fiery airfield, Bond takes cover behind nearby crates. Enemy troops disembark from a truck and an attack helicopter starts an air assault on you. There's a scoped **AK-47** on the ground where you begin the fight **(1)**. Pick it up. The helicopter flies in and starts raking the area with heavy machine gun fire. Remain covered and in between helicopter attacks, pop up and shoot the Russian soldiers.

If your cover is crumbling before you can clear the soldiers, try dashing for the concrete short wall and fence **(2)** at the corner of the hangar. Aim for the explosive barrels on the platform to take out the enemy taking cover nearby. Once you eliminate the enemies directly in front of you, dash toward the helicopter and run between the facility wall on the left and the fuel platform **(3)**. From this corner you can get a bead on the gunner on the missile platform **(4)**.

SECONDARY MISSION OBJECTIVE: NEUTRALIZE THE HELICOPTER GUNSHIP

Once the gun platform (4) is clear, run up to the top and activate the switch on the laptop to fire a single missile at the helicopter. This is one of two missile attacks that you must launch to take the helicopter down for good.

After you hit the helicopter with the first missile, three enemy guards arrive just below the gun platform. You can shoot through the missile platform rail panels. One of the gaps gives a clear shot of the truck's fuel tank. Shoot this as quickly as you can after launching the missile and you are left with one enemy hiding behind some debris. You can also take him out from behind the missile platform railing.

Follow the staircase next to the missile launcher down to the room below the platform. Here you find **Armor** and a weapon locker containing an **ANOVA DP3 + Reflex Sight** and an **AK-47 + Multiple**.

Follow the objective marker beyond the exploding and falling pipes. Work your way toward the back left corner of the platform to find a Janus symbol.

JANUS SYMBOL #9
Find this Janus symbol on the back of a shipping crate on the airfield before you reach the machine shops.

Use the Janus symbol crates for cover while you scope and shoot the distant enemies on the structure above the large hangar doors **(5)**. You should be able to defeat two soldiers on balconies and an RPG-toting soldier behind glass.

Move forward along the sidewalk on the left. Look up to the right and shoot the two soldiers on the high balcony before the doors. You can choose to go through the large hangar doors or cut through the Machine Shops **(6)** to the left through a small door at the end of the sidewalk. We suggest going through the Machine Shops.

MACHINE SHOPS

Head through the doorway at the end of the sidewalk and enter the Machine Shops **(6)**. Get the jump on the soldiers with their backs to you standing around the Humvee inside. 007 can shoot explosive barrels, which cause the broken down Humvee to detonate. Continue to mow down the reinforcements that file into the room from the stairwell or from the door leading to the next room on the right. Use the crates near the entry for cover.

Attack the adjacent room (7) (where reinforcements came from) using the lower entry or, more wisely, use the second level catwalk entry so you have the height advantage (making their cover less effective). Bond can shoot a suspended engine block, which falls and explodes.

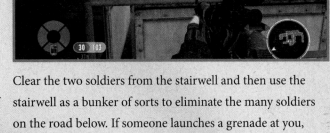

Follow the objective marker through the shop catwalks and head through a couple of doors to end up on an exterior set of stairs (8) beyond the large hangar doors (5).

Clear the two soldiers from the stairwell and then use the stairwell as a bunker of sorts to eliminate the many soldiers on the road below. If someone launches a grenade at you, dash down the stairs and take cover behind the large columns below.

JANUS SYMBOL #10

Once you are down the stairs from the machine shops and the area on the road is clear, look for this Janus symbol under a high rooftop nook near the destroyed hangar doorway.

Following the objective marker towards the air control tower places you at another hangar door passage (9) with another interior passage option. If you use the interior passage (10) to reach the next battle you have to crouch under a garage door to enter the battlefield. This is not a bad approach since you'll be closer to the missile launch pad (11) which has a nice bunker under it—a great place from which to wage your war.

Get behind the short wall barricades closest to the launch pad and take out the gunman near the doorway to the launch pad bunker. If you can't quickly take out the gunman on the launch pad, then run through the hail of bullets from the enemy soldiers and the attack helicopter that has returned to the battle.

SECOND LAUNCH PAD BUNKER

Once inside the bunker use the lookout windows to take on the remaining enemies outside and you have plenty of room to back up and get out of the way of the helicopter attack.

SECONDARY MISSION OBJECTIVE: NEUTRALIZE THE HELICOPTER GUNSHIP

Once you are safely inside the launch pad bunker **(11)**, slowly climb the stairs to the rooftop and shoot the single soldier on the rooftop, if you have not done so already. Rush to the laptop and press the button to launch the second missile at the helicopter, destroying it for good now. Be careful; there are a few soldiers on the next balcony to your left that begin firing at you. Use the stairs for cover again and make sure to find the **Armor** power-up beside the laptop.

AIR TRAFFIC CONTROL TOWER

Eliminate all the remaining enemies and then enter the tower doorway **(12)** up the stairwell behind the launching pad bunker.

As soon as you push open the door to the first floor of the control tower, look for soldiers to the left and right inside the large room. Gun down the three unsuspecting soldiers on the right first, then strafe right to take out the soldiers on the left. Find the Janus symbol in this room before heading upstairs.

JANUS SYMBOL #11

You can find this symbol stuck on the side of a filing cabinet in the back right corner of the first floor office in the control tower (12).

SECONDARY MISSION OBJECTIVE: DESTROY THE AIR TRACKING CONSOLES

Use the stairways to reach the second (13) and third floor (14) of the tower, clearing the soldiers from each small floor. Once you've defeated the enemies, begin shooting every large console on the top two floors to complete this objective.

PLANE CHASE

Head out of the tower through the second floor (13) balcony door. Bond spots his escape plane rolling down the runway. He slides down a sloped column, commandeers a motorcycle and gives chase. As soon as control returns to you, pivot to the right and shoot the two motorcycle soldiers and then focus on the plane again as the computer steers for you. Shoot the soldier that climbs out to the wing from the plane's open hatch.

Bond leaps to the edge of the hatch on the fuselage. Repeatedly bash the two indicated buttons to make Bond pull himself inside the plane. Once he stumbles to the cockpit and pushes the dead pilot away, bash the same two buttons until Bond pulls the plane up out of the nosedive to complete the mission.

MISSION 2: BARCELONA

NIGHTCLUB

PRIMARY OBJECTIVES

Locate Sergeant Garcia

Meet with Zukovsky

Escape from Zukovsky's Nightclub

SECONDARY OBJECTIVES

Obtain Zukovsky's Contact List

Photograph Zukovsky's Weapon Shipment Crates

Obtain the Nightclub Security Footage

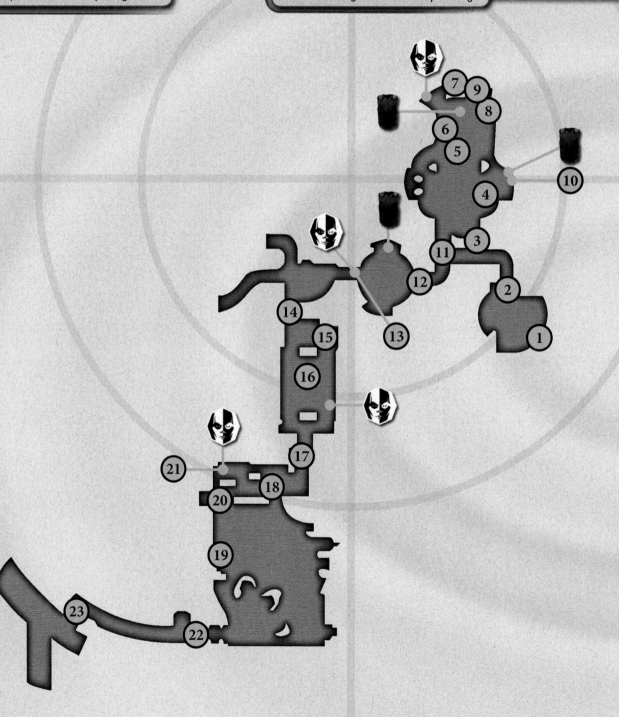

LOCATE SERGEANT GARCIA

Bond must meet with Zukovsky at his nightclub in Barcelona. Upon arriving, Bond enters **(1)** the nightclub unnoticed by the heavy security patrols. Zukovsky is located in his private office area overlooking the main dance floor. However, armed guards block your access.

Bond has a covert contact located within the club who has agreed to help him get past security to meet with Zukovsky. Armed only with the smartphone, Bond must search the club for his contact among the night club patrons.

Head up the stairs to the second level and pass through the light security at the hallway entrance **(2)**. The guard seems to think you belong at this party. Just as you enter the hallway, answer your phone to receive the message from MI6 that you can use the face-recognition app on your phone to identify Sergeant Garcia.

Follow the blip on the radar through the doors on the right (3) to enter a bar balcony overlooking the dance floor below. You receive a prompt to pull out the phone and begin scanning the targetable faces in the crowd. You don't really need it on this balcony, but pull it out anyway to get rid of the prompt and then continue down the stairs to a lower bar level (4).

ONATOPP ENCOUNTER

On this lower bar level you run into a waitress who tries to sell you some knock-off brand of vodka, trying to pass it for a much higher quality brand. This woman is Onatopp. You'll be seeing her again soon enough.

Continue down the stairwell ramp to the dance floor and make your way through the crowd to access a second level bar on the opposite side of the room. Pull out the phone and find and scan the female face of Sergeant Garcia (5).

MEET WITH ZUKOVSKY

FOLLOW SERGEANT GARCIA TO GAIN ACCESS TO ZUKOVSKY'S OFFICE.

Talk to the woman you identified as Sergeant Garcia using the facial recognition app on your smartphone. Follow her up the nearby stairs to a bodyguard (6). She gets past him but he frisks you and finds and removes your hidden P99 (which you could not equip anyway).

Follow Garcia to the open door and enter the waiting room (7) just outside Zukovsky's office. You see a guard near a stairwell in the back. He faces a Janus symbol on the side of a couch you cannot get yet without a weapon. Be sure to take the **Armor** from the couch before entering Zukovsky's office (8).

ZUKOVSKY'S OFFICE

Zukovsky and Bond talk while overlooking the nightclub through the waiting room's large observation window. Onatopp, the waitress you encountered earlier, sneaks up on the conversation and shoots Zukovsky in the back, who falls from the balcony onto the dance floor below. At least you received a quick tip about the investigation before he dies. The guests in the nightclub scatter in panic and the gunfire alerts the security guards located throughout the club, who believe Bond has killed Zukovsky. Bond must now fight his way through the different areas of the club and escape.

ESCAPE FROM ZUKOVSKY'S NIGHTCLUB

Grab the gun Onatopp intends to frame you with and then drops to the floor by your feet. Use this gun to eliminate the guards in the room. Shoot the most threatening ones first so you can dash back into Zukovsky's office to work on a side mission. It also allows you to shoot the guards through his office windows—the shooting angles from inside his office compromise their cover.

SECONDARY MISSION OBJECTIVE: OBTAIN ZUKOVSKY'S CONTACT LIST

When you reenter Zukovsky's office (8) after he is gunned down, shoot the Warhol-ish painting from the wall to reveal a safe. Open the safe and take the contact list from inside to complete this secondary objective.

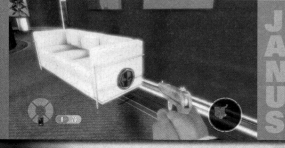

JANUS SYMBOL #12
Find this Janus symbol on the backside of the couch near the once guarded stairwell in the office waiting room. Now that you've got your hands on a weapon again, shoot this symbol.

Collect weapons from the dead and then head down the stairs (9), shoot the guy at the bottom of the stairs and take his weapon. Follow the hall to the doorway that leads back to the dance floor.

DANCE FLOOR BATTLE

When you reenter the dance floor (5), the room begins to fill with enemies. Keep an eye on both the left and right floor and balcony levels for approaching enemies. Remain near the doorway in case you need to retreat or use the nearby columns for cover. Always shoot the biggest threat first and work your way down to the least threatening. Make your way deeper through the room to reach the objective maker on the other side. Expect heavy resistance around the bar areas. Look for **Armor** behind the bar (10). Beside the Armor is a **SLY 2020** shotgun.

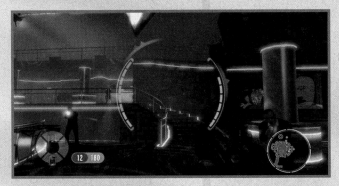

BATHROOM BREACH

Follow the objective marker on the radar out the back right hallway (11). At the end of this hallway, the intersection that leads back to the entrance is gated and locked. Follow the objective marker to a set of unlocked double doors (12). Select a fast weapon and breach the doors. Blast the initial five enemies facing you in a showdown in this bathroom area. If the slow-motion time is not long enough for you to take down all five enemies facing you, then as you shoot in slow-mo, move forward to the central counter which provides you good cover once you crouch.

While fighting in this bathroom, watch for reinforcements to arrive from the bathroom stalls on each side of the room. It's often good to rush to one side or the other and use that partition wall to protect you from gunmen on the other side of the room while you run and gun down the ones occupied on your side.

Find **Armor** and the "one-shot-you're-dead" **Wolff .44** in a bathroom stall on the right side of the room.

Follow the objective marker on the radar through the next doorway (**13**) and remain there while gunning down enemies that show themselves in the next room. Above this doorway is a Janus symbol.

JANUS SYMBOL #13

Before looking for this Janus symbol, clear out the nearby enemies. It is on the new side of the hallway, above the doorway as you leave the bathroom area.

KITCHEN

Enter the kitchen through the doorway (**14**), following the objective markers. Wait a moment in the hallway while facing the distant doorway and while not stepping in front of the windows to your left. Two enemies push through the doors at the end. Gun 'em down and then shoot the enemy in the room to your left through the window. Wait one more moment and the last gunman in the area pushes through a door to enter this glassed room and continues to find you in the hallway if you are still there. Eliminate him, take the dropped **Kallos-TT9** assault rifles and enter the room (**15**) he came out of.

Enter the backroom (15) connecting the first room on the right in the kitchen. Not only do you get to use the nice assault rifles in this room, but they are also part of the weapon shipment crates you need to photograph. Take a picture of any of the three crates in the corner (using the reticle lines to lock in a focused image) to complete this objective.

Enter the main kitchen (16) through either the initial hallway's double doors or through the next door in the weapon cache room. Use your new scoped assault rifle and shoot the enemies inside and then look for another Janus symbol in here.

JANUS SYMBOL #14
Find this Janus symbol in the kitchen (16) on the side of a crate near a corner and the exit doorway.

JANUS

Shoot the two gunmen at the kitchen exit **(17)** and then pass through the doorway to a large hallway with many doors. A secondary objective lies through the door on the right at the bottom of the short set of stairs. However, it's locked and the vent beside it is useless. Don't bother with that area now and instead head through the door on the left **(18)**.

BAR FIGHT

The gunfight in the bar is pretty serious, but you can use the bar as cover for almost the entire battle. Just duck down when you are reloading and contemplating your next target. Enemies appear all over the place in this large lounge. Keep your eyes open for a few that like to try to get behind the bar with you and those that are on high balconies that could compromise some locations behind the bar.

SECONDARY MISSION OBJECTIVE: OBTAIN THE NIGHTCLUB SECURITY FOOTAGE

Once you've cleared the room, move around it and pick up your favorite weapon choices. Head up the stairs (19) on the right side of the lounge to access the balcony. Shoot the two guards that come through the next doorway.

Enter the room (20) they came out of and find and enter the ventilation shaft in this room. Continue until you drop into a large duct conduit. Do not drop into the next hole until you shoot Janus Symbol #16 in this conduit.

Drop through the vent hole into the security room below. Use the smartphone on the node to erase the security footage and complete this secondary objective. You can now unlock the door (21) from this side to resume your main objective.

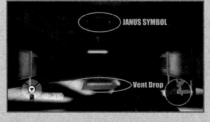 

JANUS SYMBOL #15

The last Janus symbol in this mission is located inside a vent shaft found in the ventilation conduit, just beyond the hole that drops you into the security camera footage room (21).

EXIT

After completing all the secondary objectives and finding the last of the Janus symbols in this area, follow the objective marker through the last couple of doorways **(22)**, through the long hallway, and to the exit **(23)** to complete the mission on the back of a stolen motorcycle.

WALKTHROUGH

MISSION 3: DUBAI

ARMS FAIR EXHIBITION

PRIMARY OBJECTIVES

Meet with Sky Briggs

Pursue Ourumov and Onatopp

Place a Tracking Device on the Prototype Helicopter

Escape the Frigate

SECONDARY OBJECTIVES

007 Mode and 007 Classic Mode: Rescue all Hostages (3)

007 Classic Mode: Disarm the Explosive Charges placed aboard the Frigate by Janus Men (3)

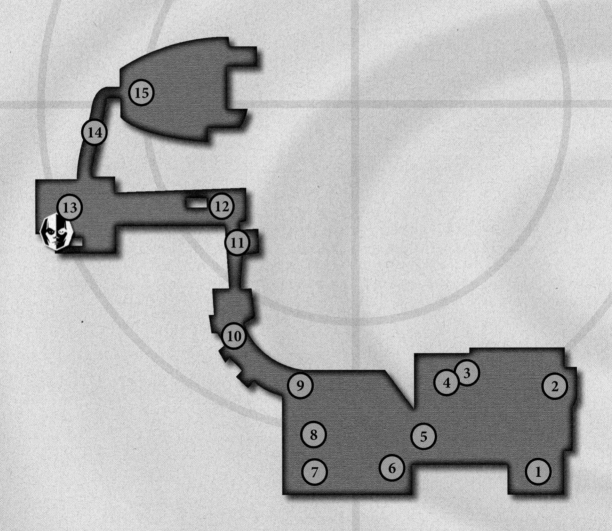

MEET WITH SKY BRIGGS

Having visited Zukovsky's Nightclub and gained information on Ourumov's whereabouts, Bond is also informed about Ourumov's right hand woman, Onatopp. Bond heads over to the weapons Exhibition in Dubai where the new prototype helicopter is being revealed.

Bond enters the exhibition during opening hours and the place is bustling with people. Bond is to meet a security contact named Sky Briggs to discuss security for the Prototype Helicopter.

Head through the entrance metal detector (1) and allow the security guard to scan you. Approach Sky Briggs (2) at the top of the balcony stairs, dead ahead. He believes there is no way anyone will try anything nefarious with the amount of security he has in place. Follow Briggs as he enters a hallway (3) and opens another door (4) to introduce you to the pilots of the helicopter.

The pilots are not in the room. He instead finds Onatopp and Ourumov pulling the triggers on the weapons aimed at him. Briggs falls dead and the pursuit is on.

PURSUE OURUMOV AND ONATOPP

PILOTS' LOUNGE

Bond produces his P99 with silencer and the enemies escape on foot through the facility. You do not need to run after them; they get away for now. Running on their heels will get you killed in the following room, as many enemy reinforcements are waiting for you in the showroom (**5**). Notice the two dead pilots on the right side of the room as you pass through the pilots' lounge (**4**).

SHOWROOM

As you enter the Showroom (**5**) many enemy guards begin to pop out from cover to shoot at you. Find a weapon case on the floor at the entrance containing a couple of **Sigmus 9's**. Shoot as many of the enemies as you can while strafing to the left, open hallway (**6**) attached to this room. Shoot the three guards that come through the double doors (**7**) in the connecting hallway. Pick up the dropped **Hawksman M5A with Silencer**.

Find the Wi-Fi node (**8**) on a counter facing a window in the second hallway. Notice that the window behind the node allows a view of the back of the showroom floor. Use your smartphone to activate this node. This activates the auto-gun placement on the showroom floor, clearing the room of enemies for you. You can join in the fun by shooting through the window at the targets that the auto-gun has not yet targeted.

Enter the showroom after all the guards are dead and fill up on weapons and ammo. Use the smartphone to hack the door lock to raise the closed roll gate **(9)**. The door lock is above the hallway balcony on the left side of the locked roll gate.

HALLWAY/STAIRS

Target and shoot the guards running toward you from the opposite end of the next hallway **(10)**. Use the advertisement stands as cover while you machine gun them all down. Head up the next set of stairs to reach the terminal **(11)**.

VIEWING GALLERY

The viewing gallery has top and bottom floors that have similar floor plans. Rush the first three enemies hiding behind the advertisement on the top floor and gun them down. Notice the remaining enemy blips originate on the lower level. There are stairs on each end of the gallery so keep an eye on the radar so no one sneaks up behind you. It's often good to rush across the top floor to the back stairwell, descend and then attack the lower level enemies from behind (they expect you from the other direction).

The end **(13)** of the lower viewing gallery level turns into a pretty big battle with reinforcements arriving through the next hallway.

JANUS SYMBOL #16

Find this Janus symbol on the underside of the luggage x-ray machine. Crouch down beside the machine so you can get a bead on it.

To avoid the metal detector alarm, climb over the ropes beside the full-body scanner and proceed down the terminal hallway (**14**). Enter the Frigate (**15**) found at the end.

FRIGATE: CONTROL DECK

As soon as you enter the ship, turn down the left hallway and find the floor ventilation shaft (**16**). Drop down inside and crouch walk forward until you see a non-functioning control panel up against a couple gated windows with a view inside the control deck. Take out your smartphone and point it through the gated window at the nearby node (**17**). This activates a ceiling auto-gun in the control deck, killing all the occupants.

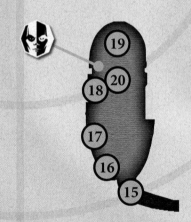

Continue following the vent to enter the back of the control deck near a set of stairs leading to an upper deck **(18)**. Silently shoot the two visible guards and then work your way around to the front of the control deck. Use the consoles for cover while you silently eliminate the remaining guards toward the back of the room to avoid reinforcements being summoned.

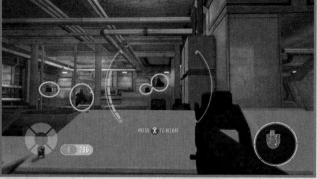

SECONDARY MISSION OBJECTIVE: DISARM EXPLOSIVE CHARGES (1/3)

This secondary objective is only available in 007 Classic mode. First, eliminate the many elite soldiers in the room. Once you've cleared the area you are ready to defuse the bomb. It is sitting on the counter near the front of the control deck on the upper level. Approach it until you receive the button prompt that defuses the bomb.

JANUS SYMBOL #17
Head to the higher platform in the back of the control deck upper level. Find the Janus symbol on the side of a counter near a locked exit.

Exit the deck through the doorway **(20)** near the Janus symbol and use the ladder in the floor hatch to reach the Mid Decks.

MID DECKS

Bond descends the ladder **(21)** from the upper deck to the mid deck just in time to see a door **(22)** shut and sealed by the fleeing targets.

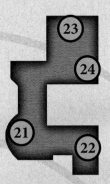

SECONDARY MISSION OBJECTIVE: RESCUE THE HOSTAGES (1/3)

Follow the objective marker to a dead-end hallway with a door you can breach (23) on the left and another floor hatch (24) with a ladder that leads down to a lower level. Breach the door with a powerful assault rifle in hand. In slow motion, shoot the hostage taker and spare the hostage to resolve the first of three hostage situations on the ship. This is only available in the two hardest game modes.

After freeing the hostage **(23)**, exit the room and take the ladder in the floor hatch **(24)** down to the lower deck.

ARMORY

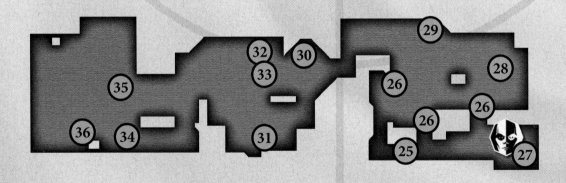

Sliding down the ladder from the mid deck places you in a hallway **(25)** on the Armory level of the frigate. This floor is made up of the hallway you are in, a large armory loading bay with three entrances **(26)** and a small hostage room **(27)** at the end. You can use a silenced weapon and attack the loading bay stealthily from behind and avoid reinforcements being deployed from further ahead.

If you instead rescue the hostage **(27)** in the secondary mission first, before attacking the loading bay, then after you shoot the hostage taker the noise alerts the enemies in the loading bay and they rush to attack. You also have to deal with reinforcements.

LOW AMMO

P99 + SILENCER

SECONDARY MISSION OBJECTIVE: RESCUE THE HOSTAGES (2/3)

Breach the doorway **(27)** on the Armory loading bay level of the frigate. Shoot the two hostage takers in slow motion mode to free the hostage.

JANUS SYMBOL #18

After freeing the hostage from the two gunmen, enter the room and look behind the door you came through. Shoot the Janus symbol from the wall behind the door.

SECONDARY MISSION OBJECTIVE: DISARM EXPLOSIVE CHARGES (2/3)

After clearing the loading bay either stealthily or in an all out gun blazing battle, find the second bomb on a console (28) near the back (where the missiles are moving to). Step up to it and defuse it by holding the indicated button. There's only one more to go to complete this objective.

98

After taking care of the enemies, the second hostage, the Janus symbol and the second bomb, move through the hallway (29) behind the loading bay and climb the set of stairs at the end to reach the engine room above.

RELEASE THE LOCKDOWN
ENGINE ROOM

At the top of the stairs you reach a short hallway with no unlocked doors. At the end of the hallway is the open engine room (30). If you have them, use silenced weapons to keep reinforcements from entering this engine room battle. Start by subduing the nearest guard overlooking the engine pit. You can see more guards beyond the pit on the opposite end of this large room. Leave them alone for now and then start moving down the left corridor. Use the consoles for cover and silently shoot the two elite soldiers with their backs to each other who are bent over working on the consoles.

TWO RELEASE NODES

There are two nodes that you must hack with your smartphone in order to release the lockdown. The first is on a console **(31)** on the left side of the engine room. After clearing the enemies from this area, point your smartphone at the control panel and hack the system. You are halfway there, as indicated by the picture on the phone.

Silently shoot the patrolling elite soldier through the next open doorway. At the same open doorway you can look down into the central engine room pit and shoot the guard messing with the next bomb.

Follow the blip on the radar down to the engine in the pit in the middle of the room. Use the smartphone on the release node on the console **(32)** on the side of the turbine. This quiets the alarm and cancels the lockdown.

SECONDARY MISSION OBJECTIVE: DISARM EXPLOSIVE CHARGES (3/3)

The third and final bomb (33) you need to defuse is on the end of the same turbine that housed the second lockdown release node. Defuse the bomb as you did the others to complete this secondary mission.

CARGO HOLD

When you open the cargo hold door (34) you spot three unsuspecting elite soldiers. There are two others you can't see from the doorway, inside the room behind some crates. Use a silenced weapon to shoot the two closest ones on the floor ahead of you, followed by the soldier on the back catwalk. Stealthily shoot the third and fourth soldier near the lift on the first floor (seen standing near a large stack of crates). By taking these five out stealthily you avoid having to battle reinforcements.

Follow the catwalk around the large equipment lift and activate the *cargo lift override* switch on the console (35) blipped on the radar as your current objective location.

The lift (36) lowers with a vehicle and three elite soldiers firing assault rifles at you. If you just target the vehicles you can cause them to explode before the troops can spread out into the room. If you missed this opportunity and they all begin attacking, you cannot stay in the control room for long. If you didn't already eliminate them, the three elite soldiers soon start tossing grenades inside. Escape to the floor and shoot through the barricade crates.

Leap over the single crate in the barricade. As you do, three more elite soldiers enter the room and begin their attack up on the catwalk. These guys are extremely aggressive. You can use the cover near the lift or jump back over the barricade crates behind you to reach even better cover. Gun down the three soldiers and then get on the lift and activate the switch (36) to ride up to the helipad.

PLACE A TRACKING DEVICE ON THE PROTOTYPE HELICOPTER

As the cargo lift (**36**) reaches the top, the prototype helicopter (**37**) is just preparing to take off—stolen by Onatopp and Ourumov. Bond must place his tracking device on it as it escapes. To do this quickly, find the opening in the lift railing (the chopper nose points at the opening). Quickly pass through this opening and approach the helicopter. Bond automatically grasps the underside as the helicopter lifts off the pad. Press the Vault button to place the smartphone on the chopper. Bond drops to the ground and the chopper begins shooting at him. Gun down the two soldiers at the next doorway (38), allowing you access back inside the frigate (38) for cover from the helicopter that continues to attack.

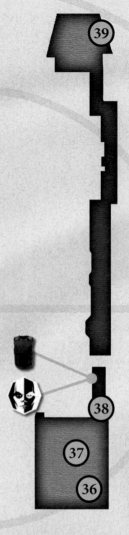

ESCAPE THE FRIGATE
ESCAPE CORRIDOR

Bond must now run through a doorway and escape the ship. As he passes through the corridors the helicopter shoots the side of the ship. Flames sprout from areas, pillars collapse and a variety of other damage occurs around him. Take the **Armor** from the floor in the first nook on the left in the corridor.

JANUS SYMBOL #19
When you stop to pick up the Armor from the burning nook in the corridor, look up above the computer console on the wall in the nook. Here you find the last Janus symbol in this mission. The frigate is rocking so you may find it easier to shoot it from the hip as opposed to looking down the sight.

Continue dodging bullets while just activating sprint after sprint to quickly get to safety. Eventually you end up in the starting area below the control room **(39)**. Shoot the one remaining soldier and as everything collapses around you, rush for the only exit, directly ahead. As Bond exits this room the area of the ship's side marked in red explodes, Bond dives into the water below and the level ends.

MISSION 4: SEVERNAYA

OUTPOST

SEVERNAYA, SIBERIA

PRIMARY OBJECTIVES

Track Your Smartphone

Find the Lower Compound

Avoid the Crossfire

Infiltrate the Lower Compound

Navigate the Tunnel

Enter the Bunker

SECONDARY OBJECTIVES

Find the Supply Crates (6)

Take Black Box from Crashed MIG (007 Classic Mode only)

TRACK YOUR SMARTPHONE

MI6 reports that an hour ago the EMP Hardened Helicopter landed at a remote base in Siberia. A distress signal was heard from that location 25 minutes ago on military channels. The Russians have sent in combat troops and two MIGs. Bond's job is to avoid the troops and infiltrate the base to find out what they are up to.

In the beginning (**1**) of the mission you are armed with nothing more than your silenced P99. Your phone, if you remember, is on the helicopter. Track the signal from your smartphone hidden onboard the stolen prototype helicopter. Follow the patrolling guard using the lower narrow route on the edge of the map and come up behind the soldier (**2**) and subdue him. Take his silenced **Sigmus**.

Follow the continuing trail up the hill and slowly veer left toward where the other two guards stand facing each other (**3**). Silently shoot them in quick succession to avoid detection. Take their weapons and continue toward the objective marker.

Subdue the lone soldier (**4**) just before a small bridge over the path. He has his back to you and is therefore an easy target. Remain where you are and allow the two soldiers on the bridge (**5**) to show themselves. While they are talking to each other, silently shoot them both in quick succession.

JANUS SYMBOL #20

*This Janus symbol is located under the left arch (slightly up the hill) of the bridge (**5**) where you took out the two soldiers talking next to the truck.*

Remain under the bridge (**5**) and look further up the path to an overturned tree, making its own bridge. Silently shoot the solder on this dead tree before he turns in your direction during his patrol.

Upon reaching the end of the trail (**6**) there is a sudden EMP attack on the facility on the mountain peak. Russian enemies and vehicles are crossing the bridge when suddenly a MIG falls from the Sky and collides with the bridge. Bond tries to make a call to MI6 but fails, just before a helicopter falls from the sky, nearly crushing Bond. Bond rolls off the cliff and blacks out.

FIND THE LOWER COMPOUND

As soon as you come to, you notice a blinking "i" icon on the screen and see a large troop of soldiers in the next clearing. The burning helicopter rests in a tree just above your head. You now have a secondary objective and the first stage can be solved in this little beginning pathway (7).

SECONDARY MISSION OBJECTIVE: FIND THE SUPPLY CRATES (1/6)

From your starting position, pivot to the right and find the dark weapon chest with the padlock on it in a little nook. If you don't want to risk alerting the nearby soldiers, hit the padlock with the butt of your gun, as if subduing an enemy.

BIGGER ISN'T ALWAYS BETTER

You must decide to take or leave the weapons you find in the hidden weapon chests. We prefer to get through as much of this level as possible using stealth, so holding onto the silenced weapons is recommended.

Crouch walk up behind the log at the clearing. Subdue the guard with his back to you by pulling him over the log and slugging him.

A non-stop march of enemy soldiers appears on the bridge before you. To avoid detection, move around the extreme left edge of this clearing and come up behind the soldier with his back to you at the snowmobile (8). Subdue him and then subdue the soldier with his back to you in the middle bridge tunnel section.

Move into the right most tunnel under the bridge and slowly crouch-walk up to the exit area and stop when you see a soldier leaning up against a wall, looking like he's getting sick **(9)**. Put him out of his misery by silently putting a round in his head.

Continue along the right wall and come up behind the soldier just outside of the tunnel, leaning up against a large, chopped tree trunk. Subdue him **(10)**. Notice the two soldiers in the distance near a large fire. Avoid them for now by reentering the tunnel.

When reentering the tunnel, move through the middle, entering the middle section and stopping near a column that separates the next section where you spot a soldier near a sparking fuse box. Silently shoot him in the head and if the patrolling guard has arrived near him, shoot him quickly after to avoid detection.

If you are discovered at this point, control the chaos by quickly shooting the remaining two guards **(11)** near the fire. If you're quick enough, only two others arrive from further ahead to reinforce these troops.

SECONDARY MISSION OBJECTIVE: FIND THE SUPPLY CRATES (2/6)

In the leftmost tunnel section you can find an open crate with Armor. Across from that crate is a padlocked supply crate. Shoot it open.

The next alley of destruction left by the downed MIG seems kind of tough at first, as a large number of troops patrol along the left side of the debris. All you need to worry about is the one soldier that walks out onto the metal scrap bridge and inspects the wreckage. Crouch-walk the entire way and subdue him when he **(12)** jumps down into your trench.

Drop down onto the ledge below at the end of the trench where the objective marker sits. Remain on this ledge and take in the next area. There's an overturned vehicle with a soldier near a snowmobile just beyond that. Put a single silenced P99 bullet in his head by shooting over the overturned truck.

Move a little further and a new set of enemies appears on the radar. One comes running out of the nearby tunnel toward the truck. Crouch walk to the truck and when the guard passes the right end of the truck, crouch walk up behind him and subdue him **(13)**. Return to hiding behind the truck.

Three soldiers remain in the area. Two near the entrance to the next tunnel and another on an overturned tree above the tunnel entrance **(14)**. Watch them from around the front of the overturned truck. When the one guard at the tunnel walks away from the other, snipe the guard that remains at the tunnel by putting a silenced round in his head. Then quickly do the same to the guard above him on the felled tree. Shoot or subdue the remaining soldier that wandered off to the left.

SECONDARY MISSION OBJECTIVE: FIND THE SUPPLY CRATES (3/6)

You can find this supply crate on the opposite side of the overturned truck. Shoot the lock off once the area is clear of enemies.

AVOID THE CROSSFIRE

Follow the trail until you see a red flare on the pathway ahead. Stop and look for the soldiers on the pathway near the flare **(15)**. Shoot the soldier and anyone else that comes to his rescue. The Russian base is under attack from an unidentified force. Avoid the crossfire here and continue to the compound.

There are soldiers on a bridge road above and opposing forces on cliff tops above you, but the only soldiers you really need to worry about are those that are on your pathway. Shoot the soldier behind the bolder near the bridge. When you approach the small, dilapidated bridge **(16)** a truck explodes from a rocket attack and rolls off the taller bridge. No worries. It won't hit you. Shoot the soldiers on the opposite side of the bridge from behind cover of the large boulder. Sprint across the bridge and to the next objective marker to escape the mayhem.

INFILTRATE THE LOWER COMPOUND

You climb a narrow pathway up a short hill. As you crest the hill you see a scorched pathway through some trees and leading into a military camp ahead. A full-scale battle is taking place between the Russian and Janus forces and you can use this to your advantage. Both factions are so busy with each other that they won't notice you. That is, until they are hit by your bullets or if you get too close. So, if you continue to silently headshot those that are close or if you walk far enough away from them, you can continue through this crazy war scene without having to take everyone out.

You must find a way into the Monorail building and make your way up to the peak. When you reach the first broken column (**18**) in the middle of the scorching, you discover a new secondary objective: Find the Black Box. Don't leave the area without this. It's not far.

Shoot the soldiers from the left porch of the burnt shell of a building ahead (**19**). Clear the soldiers that seem interested in you and then pass through the burnt shell and stop at the exit. You see some soldiers pass through the storage container (**20**) outside. Allow them to take their positions in the battle with the opposing force and then silently pop their heads. One soldier is at the container and the other two are behind the next two low cover positions.

114

Slowly exit the burnt building and walk behind the storage container (**20**). Stop at the back edge of the container and shoot two of the three soldiers taking positions near the next building to fire at the enemies on top of the dam-like structure. The third soldier heads to the top floor of the building (**21**).

SECONDARY MISSION OBJECTIVE: FIND THE SUPPLY CRATES (4/6)

You can find this supply crate on the bottom floor of the satellite building (21) near the front door. Shoot the padlock.

JANUS SYMBOL #21
This Janus symbol is located on the second floor of the interior satellite building (21). Find it on the wall under the windows and a desk.

You can find a **WA2000** sniper rifle on the top of the satellite building **(21)**. To get there, pass through the second floor to the exterior balcony. Follow the balcony around to the rooftop stairs. Crouch down and take the rifle out of the chest near the dead soldier. Use this weapon to clear a few of the soldiers in the middle area of the camp, as you eventually need to pass by that area.

SECONDARY MISSION OBJECTIVE: TAKE BLACK BOX FROM CRASHED MIG (CLASSIC MODE ONLY)

You can find the black box under the wing of the crashed MIG as you exit the satellite building (21).

Follow the scorched trail created by the downed MIG. Prepare to gun down a soldier that passes through the next storage container **(22)**. Enter the container and from the exit, shoot the soldier on the front porch of the radio cabin **(23)**.

SECONDARY MISSION OBJECTIVE: FIND THE SUPPLY CRATES (5/6)

Clear the radio building of enemies and find the supply crate on the floor between bunks. The weapon inside is a **Kallos-TT9 with Grenade Launcher**. This can be very useful in the completion of this mission.

JANUS SYMBOL #22

*Exit the radio building (23) and climb the guard tower ladder to reach the shelter above. You can find a **sniper rifle** up here and can spend some time here sniping soldiers, but the best thing to do is shoot the Janus symbol on the interior wall and get out before a rocket is shot at you.*

Make a beeline for the guardhouse (24) and use the areas below the windows for cover. Pop up and shoot the guards that take an interest in your current position. Once you've eliminated the guards around the nearby truck at the gate and the Humvee near the downed MIG, sprint for the objective marker inside the burning building (25).

Follow the burning hallway through the debris to find the ventilation shaft at the top of a pile of rubble in the back left corner of this area.

NAVIGATE THE TUNNEL

Follow the ventilation shaft to the exit (26). Take the vent cover off and then silently headshot each of the approaching soldiers below in quick succession. There's a third soldier with his back to you further ahead. Drop down into the new room.

Take the **WA2000 + Thermal Scope** from the gun rack near the fallen soldiers. Take the **Armor** from the rack as well. As you approach the third guard standing with his back to you at the burning, upside-down tramcar, you see a laser tracking into the room from the distance and your target drops at your feet. Good thing you grabbed that sniper rifle.

Select the WA2000, reload it and step into the upside-down tramcar **(27)**. Do not walk any further than the entrance, remaining on the lower end of the slopped floor near the rooftop dent. Crouch down and begin looking through the scope through the top edge of the tram exit and out into the distant room. From this location you can snipe two snipers perched high in the next room without them spotting you.

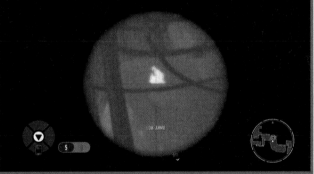

As you move out of the tramcar, three more enemies appear in that distant room. Grab an assault rifle and pick them off using the pile of fallen wall as cover. Notice the locked double doors to your left. Two enemy soldiers breach this door moments after you kill the last soldier in the next chamber. This breach is accompanied by a flashbang. If you get caught up in this, you're pretty much dead. So, as soon as you kill the third soldier, back up into the inside of the tram. Head deep inside and look away from the blast. When you hear the explosion, start shooting the two soldiers through the tram windows.

Enter the next room and follow the hallway to the ventilation shaft. Follow the ventilation to one of two exits. (It doesn't matter which you choose). Pop off the vent cover and drop down into the turbine (28).

ENTER THE BUNKER

Entering the area through a large ventilation fan, Bond finds the Janus forces setting up a defensive perimeter, which he must sneak or break through to reach the main entrance into the facility itself.

Before exiting the turbine (28), look out into the open area ahead. Spot the nearest soldier almost looking in your direction behind a short wall. Silently put a bullet in his head and then sprint out of the turbine and turn right. Follow the catwalk down into a shelter (29).

SECONDARY MISSION OBJECTIVE: FIND THE SUPPLY CRATES (6/6)

Find the last supply crate on the ground in the shelter at the beginning of the helicopter area. You can also find a nearby **rocket launcher** and **Armor** in an adjacent chest.

JANUS SYMBOL #23

Find the last Janus symbol in this mission stuck up high on the large satellite dish above the bunker. Use a sniper rifle or you can shoot it silently with your P99 from the safety of the shelter (22).

Move up to the rocks **(30)** and crouch down. Your next couple of targets appear on the left side of the area. There are two soldiers behind the burning pipe ahead. Silently shoot these guards in the head.

If you alert the enemy you can always back up to the shelter and use the large columns for cover as you gun down your pursuers. Your next most important target is the sniper in the back left tower **(31)**. Use cover and a sniper rifle to take him out.

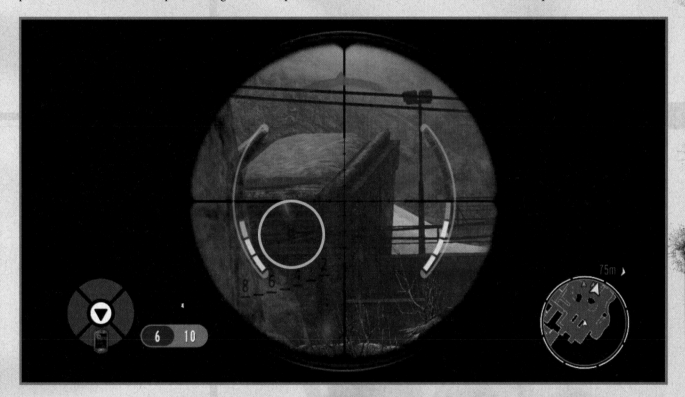

If you enter the sniper tower you can use the shelter **(31)** as a great place to eliminate many attacking soldiers. Once all the enemies in the area are gone, sprint for the bunker's main entrance **(32)** and pry the doors apart while bashing the indicated buttons.

PRIMARY OBJECTIVES

- Investigate the Bunker
- Locate the Power Generator
- Enter the Server Room
- Neutralize Ourumov's Men
- Follow the Device
- Escape the Bunker
- Follow the Russian Girl

SECONDARY OBJECTIVES

- Gather Intel from the Bunker (5)
- Disarm Explosive Charges (5)

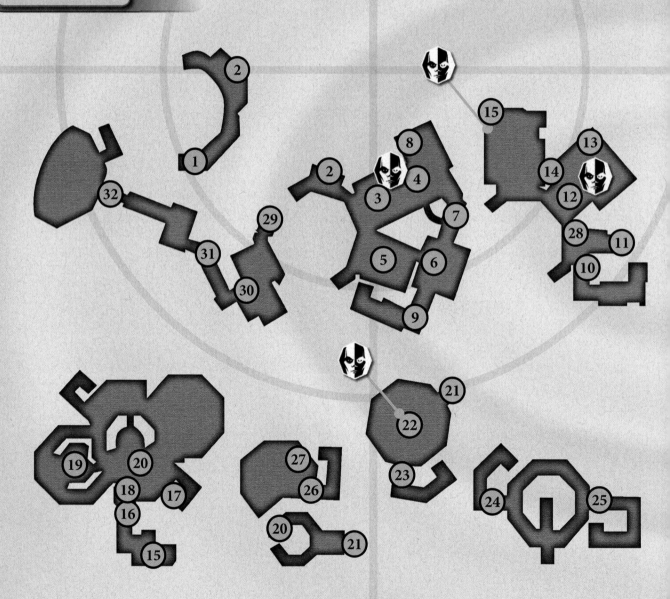

INVESTIGATE THE BUNKER

LEVEL 3

Bond has reached the interior of the Severnaya Facility and must now investigate the base to discover what happened. Ouromov and his men are still here and are cleaning up the base of any evidence or survivors while trying to gain access to the GoldenEye Key. Bond starts looking around the main room, watching Ouromov and Onatopp discuss the situation in the server room.

You begin on the third level balcony (1) in the bunker. Move to the staircase (2) and stop on the second or third step. Look down to the three soldiers on the lower level. Two soldiers walk away together while the third walks to a bomb on the wall at the bottom of the stairs. Subdue the guard at the bottom of the stairs. He's too preoccupied with the bomb to notice you.

LEVEL 2

SECONDARY MISSION OBJECTIVE: DISARM EXPLOSIVE CHARGES (1/5)

The first bomb is located on a wall at the bottom of the first set of stairs you come to. Subdue the soldier who's messing with the bomb. Step up to the bomb to activate the defuse prompt and hold the indicated button to do the deed.

Pick up the dead soldier's **Strata SV-400** and crouch walk up to the first room on the left (3). As you peek into the room you see a soldier hitting a piece of equipment. On the radar you spot another five soldiers in the room and others in the next adjacent room. Subdue the soldier near the door who has his back to you.

Look around the corner of the equipment cabinet the soldier was beating on. In the back left corner of the room is another soldier messing with stuff he's probably not qualified to mess with. Pop him in the head with a silent round.

Crouch walk to the front right corner and quickly subdue the soldier facing the corner of the room. Move back to the entry area to avoid being spotted by the remaining three guards deeper in the room.

Climb over the obstruction where the first guard in this room was located and then make your way to the back corner where the second guard you killed was standing. Now silently shoot the soldier you can see facing an equipment cabinet on the raised platform (4) in the back of the room.

Stand at the hollow cabinet that contains a Janus symbol and look through it toward the stairs to the platform in the back of the room. A patrolling guard enters your view. Silently shoot him in the head. Don't shoot the Janus symbol until you've cleared the area of enemies. Maneuver around the room and silently shoot the remaining soldier on the platform in the back of the room.

JANUS SYMBOL #24

After clearing the room (3) of enemies, find and shoot the Janus symbol located inside the hollow equipment on the lower floor in the back left corner (facing the inside from the hallway entrance).

Head back out of the room and reenter the hallway. Walk further down the hallway to find the second room on the left. The room (5) is full of enemies and a bomb. Don't even bother with stealth here. Just use an assault rifle from the protection of the doorway and fill anyone that exposes themselves full of lead. You find a padlocked weapon chest in the dark, dead-end of the hallway just outside of this room. There's a **Strata SV-400 + Reflex Sight** that serves you well. Clear the room and then enter.

Enter the room (5) and leap over the handrail ahead of you. A bomb is located on a wall to your left as you vault over the rail.

SECONDARY MISSION OBJECTIVE: DISARM EXPLOSIVE CHARGES (2/5)

The second bomb is located in the second room on the level 2 hallway. Once you clear the room, enter and leap over the handrail. You can find the bomb on the wall to your left near the railing. Defuse it.

Enter the next room (6) and clear any enemies in the area. You soon notice that the back hallway (7) connects the original room (4) via a ventilation shaft and a doorway. Continue into the previous room (4) using either passageway. Enter the last unexplored room (8) on this level via the back door in room (4). Shoot the two soldiers that you see through the door window once inside the burning room.

SECONDARY MISSION OBJECTIVE: GATHER INTEL FROM THE BUNKER (1/5)

The first intel to photograph is located in this burning room (8). Look through your smartphone and you find the blue frame reticle directing you to the exact location. The blueprints that you need to capture are on a table, facing the fire in the corner.

Shoot the padlock from the door for another way into the previous hallway **(7)**. Two guards patrol this hallway now. Remain in the room until you see that they have approached and are now walking away. Silently shoot the lagger in the back and then follow the other to the end of the hallway and eliminate him.

TAKE THEM ALL OUT!

*If you raise an alert here, many soldiers fill the connecting room **(6)** and some open the door to the hallway to attack. If this happens, stand near the servers for protection and aim at the door, shooting anyone that opens it. When no more are brave enough to do that, enter the room and clear out the remaining enemies.*

Follow the objective makers through the room, down a set of stairs (defeat the soldier there), **(9)** through a hallway and down to a breach door **(10)** on level 1.

LEVEL 1

Breach the doorway **(10)** and shoot the two soldiers inside in slo-mo. The hostage turns out to be Natalya. At first she is frightened of you. You are dressed like them to blend in. Bond tries to win her trust and she runs off through a doorway that is soon inaccessible due to a falling beam.

LOCATE THE POWER GENERATOR

Approach the door indicated by the objective marker and turn on your night vision goggles (up on the D-pad) to navigate through the darkness. In the first corner you can find a **Kallos-TT9 + Laser Pointer** on the floor. Pivot to your right here and you find a switch blinking on the wall. Press the indicated button to throw the toggle switch **(11)**. This unlocks a new door.

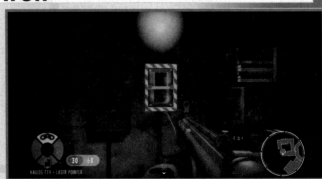

124

CONTINUE THE INVESTIGATION

Backtrack once again and disengage the night vision goggles. The door (10) is unlocked and you can see guards on the other side through the door window. Watch the patrol route of the enemies on the other side of the door. Open the door when you have the advantage. Shoot the two soldiers in this next hallway.

SECONDARY MISSION OBJECTIVE: DISARM EXPLOSIVE CHARGES (3/5)

The third bomb is located at the end of the hallway you reach just after throwing the switch in the dark room. You can find a soldier working on the bomb when you discover it. Shoot him and then disarm the bomb.

Follow the objective marker to the second doorway on the right (12), the first being the door you just used. Turn on the night vision goggles and begin attacking the soldiers in the dark room ahead. The room is full of enemies. Be patient and be on the look out for grenades and be ready to run. Once you've taken them all out, head for the objective marker in the back left corner (13).

PRESS **X** TO RELOAD

JANUS SYMBOL #25

The next Janus symbol can be found in the dark room (13) where you battle many soldiers while using the night vision goggles. The symbol is on the inside of a ramshackle desk and cubical near the fire.

Following the objective marker you enter a narrow hallway in the room close to the fire. If you haven't done so already, clear the two soldiers from inside this hallway. Follow the path up some rubble and to a closed door with a window **(14)**.

Enter the next room while crouched. Silently shoot the three soldiers in the various locations in the office area. Notice the smartphone indicator is lit. There's another intel photo op nearby.

SECONDARY MISSION OBJECTIVE: GATHER INTEL FROM THE BUNKER (2/5)

The second piece of intel to photograph is located in the office in the studded area in the corner. The blueprint is on a table. Take a pic with your smartphone.

Follow the objective marker to a set of double doors. Pry these doors open by quickly bashing the indicated button. Enter the elevator shaft **(15)**.

JANUS SYMBOL #26
Before dropping down through the elevator access hatch, look up into the elevator shaft above and find the Janus symbol on the side wall.

Drop down through the elevator access hatch and notice the solider in the next hallway with his back to you. Silently shoot that guy in the head and cautiously move out of the elevator (15) when his sidekick in the hallway moves into view. Silently shoot him and then exit the lift.

Head through the debris to the objective marker (16) at the end of the hallway. Stop at the end of the hallway and silently shoot the soldier with his back to you looking over the balcony.

Head straight out to the balcony from the hallway and look down over the edge. You can spot four enemies below. Two are near a large holograph globe in the center of the room and two are patrolling the outskirts. Use a silenced weapon to shoot the two patrolling soldiers first and then shoot the two near the globe in quick succession to remain stealthy.

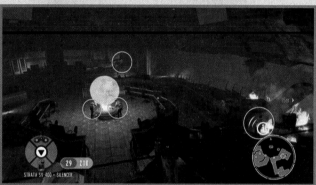

Follow the objective marker down the nearby stairwell (17) to reach that lower level now. Turn left as you exit the stairwell and silently shoot the nearby guard on the left. Continue following the walkway to the left and subdue the soldier near the stairs with his back to you (18).

SECONDARY MISSION OBJECTIVE: DISARM EXPLOSIVE CHARGES (4/5)

You can find the fourth bomb on the wall at the stairs you take to reach the upper deck where three soldiers are located.

Follow the stairs next to the fourth bomb up to the upper deck. Stop at the top of the stairs so you can see over the counter. Silently shoot the three soldiers on the deck (**19**).

SECONDARY MISSION OBJECTIVE: GATHER INTEL FROM THE BUNKER (3/5)

The third intel photo op is located on the deck overlooking the holograph globe. Look for the blueprints on the counter after you defeat the three soldiers.

SECONDARY MISSION OBJECTIVE: GATHER INTEL FROM THE BUNKER (4/5)

The fourth piece of intel you need to photograph is located on the desktop near the holograph globe in the middle of the room. It's a good idea to clear the three soldiers from the upper deck (19) overlooking this area before you try to take a picture of this blueprint.

ENTER THE SERVER ROOM

The next objective marker appears on the narrow stairwell (**20**) near the holograph globe. Follow the stairs downward. Along the way you spot a Janus symbol on the central column behind bulletproof glass. Remember that it is there; you can shoot it when you get to a lower level.

SECONDARY MISSION OBJECTIVE: DISARM EXPLOSIVE CHARGES (4/5)

The next objective marker (**21**) begs you to turn left into the next hallway, but if you continue around the central glass enclosure you spot a soldier near the last bomb you need to diffuse. Shoot the soldier and disarm the explosive stuck on the wall at the end of the walkway.

Follow the objective marker (**21**) to the closed double doors. Pry the doors open and enter the elevator. If you did not start any alerts then you receive the achievement "Invisible Descent" when the elevator doors close behind you. To get moving, pull the emergency handle to the right of the elevator doors. This abruptly drops the lift down to the next level.

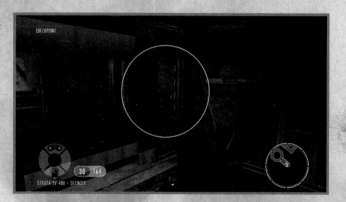

NEUTRALIZE OURUMOV'S MEN
SERVER ROOM

When the elevator doors open on the Server Room **(22)** level, shoot the two nearest soldiers and try to quickly get a fix on the third, more distant soldier behind the central column before he takes cover. The fourth enemy can also be found behind the central column.

The Server Room is similar to a battle arena. You have to clear a single wave of enemies in the beginning and then pull the lever to the left of the doors across the room **(23)**. When this is done, all hell breaks loose and you have to battle what seems like a non-stop influx of soldiers. Begin by making the sniper on the catwalk near the central column your priority target and then shoot from the hip until you can sprint to back to the previous elevator **(21)**.

Unless you are good with using the columns and short walls for cover, get back to the elevator as quickly as possible to use the inside doorway for cover from all the enemies that spawn and continue to spawn as you take out more enemies.

JANUS SYMBOL #26
The final Janus symbol in this mission is located on near the top of the central column in the server room. You saw it earlier, before taking the elevator down to this level, but you could not shoot it through the bulletproof glass. Now there are no obstructions. Shoot it.

FOLLOW THE DEVICE

Once all the enemies in the server room have been eradicated, follow the objective marker into the open hallway (23). Follow the stairs to the top level and shoot the guard that's running into the next area (24).

Remain at the doorway entrance to this upper level until no more soldiers seek you out. Use the doorway for cover as you shoot those that run out from cover. Clear the room of enemies and inspect the small cabin inside the central column in the middle of the room. Inside is the final blueprint.

SECONDARY MISSION OBJECTIVE: GATHER INTEL FROM THE BUNKER (5/5)

The final blueprint to photograph is located in the small room inside the central column above the server room.

Follow the objective marker to the next open hallway (25) and shoot the two soldiers near the large fire. Continue up the stairs to reach a checkpoint. Through the next set of doors (26) is your new objective. This objective has you running all the way back through the level to the location where you entered the facility while destroying any soldiers that stand in your way.

ESCAPE THE BUNKER

Throw the switch to the left of the sliding metal doors (26). Shoot the occupants of the next room. Remain near the doorway until a few soldiers have run down the stairs from the upper level to attack. Clear them out and then enter the room.

If you follow the objective marker up the set of stairs indicated on the radar you walk right into a sniper trap. Instead, head up the stairs (27) on the opposite side of the room near the entrance so you can get a bead on the snipers before they take you out.

From the top of the stairs with the rubble close to your left you can inch your way out into the open to spot the source of the sniper rifle laser. The sniper is on a balcony to the left under the broken catwalk bridge above (#1). As soon as you shoot the sniper another appears on a balcony one level above and a little to the left (#2). Inch out a little further and shoot him. The third sniper (#3) appears to the far right in the highest right balcony. Shoot him and continue through the objective marker on the walkway.

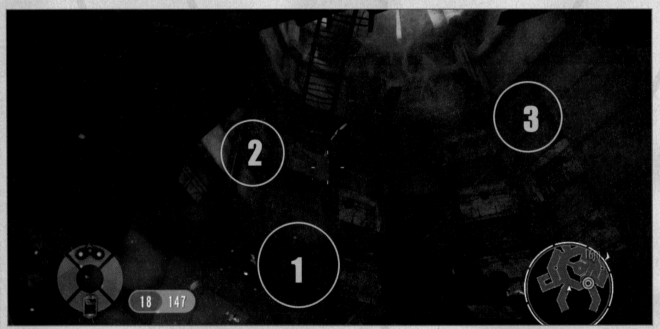

From here on out you backtrack through the entire bunker, defeating enemies around almost every corner. You should have collected all the Janus symbols and completed the secondary objectives, so you only have to concentrate on staying alive. Although the place seems to be coming apart, you do not have a time limit to get out. So, take your time so you don't run headlong into groups of enemies. Simply follow the objective markers to find the way out if you don't recognize the areas while moving through the level in reverse.

When you reach the open chasm again (**17**), remain in the stairwell until two soldiers rush the entrance. Shoot them both and head left through the burning hallway. Sprint to avoid the snipers in the chasm. You deal with them shortly. At the wrecked elevator (**15**), enter the shaft and navigate the boards to avoid a pitfall and climb the ladder to the next level up.

When you reach the dark room in flames (where you found Janus symbol #25) avoid using the nightvision goggles since the enemies stand in front of bright flames. Remain near the entry and use the door (**14**) for cover while taking out all your foes. A large explosion occurs in this room, dropping obstructions in your path. You must vault over a fallen beam (**13**) between spots of fire to reach an exit.

When you reenter the chasm balcony outside of the rooms, shoot the two guards to the left and watch as a large explosion destroys the next door you need to pass through (**28**). Repeatedly press the two indicated buttons to move the debris so you can enter the room.

Once inside the room, turn to your right and find the small hole in the double doors (**10**) accented by a fallen beam. When you pass through, you reach a checkpoint. Head to the top of the stairs and shoot the two soldiers (**9**) in the back that are running in the same direction you are headed.

As you crest the stairs leading into the lab (**6**), four soldiers run into the room from a doorway on the left side of the room. Use a grenade launcher or just shoot them in quick succession with an assault rifle before they find positions to shoot from.

Shoot the three soldiers that rush into the next room (**5**). If you beat them to the stairs at the entrance walkway then you can just mow them down as they round the corner into this burning room. Stop at the doorway and shoot the two guards that zipline into the hallway.

Across the chasm are two rocket-launching soldiers. If you stick around here too long one of their rockets finds you. You can't survive that. You may be able to quickly take them out from behind the cover at the entrance of this room, but it's a good idea to sprint out of the room heading right, and shoot the soldier that jumps out into the hallway from the next room (**3**).

RUN FROM THE ROCKETS

If the rockets are flying, don't take the time to subdue the guard.

An explosion blocks the hallway. Run up the stairs (**2**) and use the column to the left of the broken catwalk bridge for cover as you maneuver yourself to see the two snipers on the balconies on your level across the chasm. Shoot them before they snipe you.

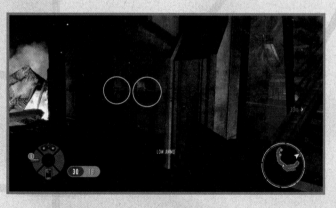

Walk out onto the catwalk bridge a few steps and look down and to the left. Find and shoot the rocket-launching soldier on the balcony a level below yours. There's one more rocket-launching soldier on the right side. Come out further on the bridge while looking down to your right. Shoot the soldier and run to the objective marker at the end of the broken catwalk bridge.

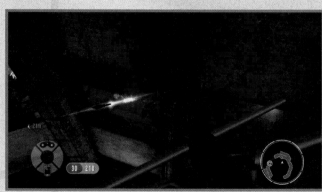

Open the ventilation cover from the ventilation shaft **(29)** to the left of the large fan at the end of the catwalk bridge.

Follow the objective marker through the next room and to the nearby hallway where you run into Natalya. Bond calls her out on setting off the distress signal. She admits to it. This completes the current objective and begins another…

FOLLOW THE RUSSIAN GIRL

Follow Natalya over a fallen column **(31)** and through the continuing hallway, crouch walking under the next obstruction. Follow her up a small debris ramp and climb up the rubble to the right of this to drop down to the floor ahead.

Vault over the rubble to reach the next hallway and start sprinting after Natalya. Help her pry open the exit **(32)**.

MISSION 5: ST. PETERSBURG

PRIMARY OBJECTIVES

Pursue Ourumov and Escape the Military Archives

SECONDARY OBJECTIVES

Recover the Interrogation Recording

Destroy the Servers

Gather Russian Intelligence for MI6 (3)

PURSUE OURUMOV AND ESCAPE THE MILITARY ARCHIVES

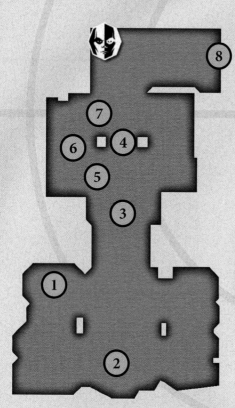

BASEMENT CELLS

Bond and Natalya are being held in a sparsely furnished cell (**1**), awaiting interrogation from Defense Minister Mishkin. During the encounter, Ourumov hurriedly enters and assassinates Mishkin and a guard, with the pretense of pinning the murders on Bond. Ourumov quickly escorts Natalaya from the cell and instructs nearby guards to kill Bond. Grabbing the weapon from the defeated guard, Bond must now pursue the fleeing Ourumov and escape the Archives.

With Ourumov's hurried departure and the sounds of gunfire, the Military Archives have gone into lockdown. All guards are on full alert, with instructions to kill Bond on sight. With a selection of multiple routes available to Bond, he must battle his way through the archives, amidst the chaos and destruction around him. Using whatever means necessary, even if it means blasting through walls, Bond must escape and continue his pursuit of Ourumov.

Bond automatically picks up the AK-47 and is placed in the nearby hallway (**2**), looking down the barrel at two guards trying to take cover behind tables at the bottom of the next set of stairs (**3**). Gun them down and then slowly climb the stairs and shoot the two guards through the bars in the next room (**4**).

The place is locked down. There are doors (**5**) on both sides of the hallway, each leading to interrogation rooms with breakable glass (**6**). Choose one way to go and break the glass inside, climb into the next room and gain entry to the area beyond the locked gates by passing through the unlocked door (**7**).

JANUS

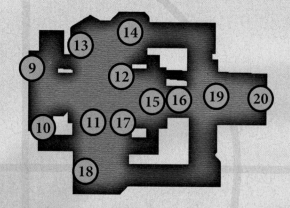

JANUS SYMBOL #28
The first Janus symbol in this mission is on the side of the crates at the bottom of the stairs, found just after breaking the interrogation room glass (7).

SECURITY CHECKPOINT

After shooting the nearby Janus symbol, shoot the two guards at the top of the next set of stairs **(8)**. Climb the stairs and shoot who you can through the two layers of bars between you and the enemies in the control room.

140

To get beyond this locked gate, again there are two options: ventilation shafts (9) & (10) on each side of the hallway. If you take the right vent (10) then when you exit you are face to face with an enemy gunman. If you take the left vent, you have a wall nook between you and this gunman at the next door (11).

Remain in the hallway until a second gunman exits the control room door (11). Gun him down and then enter the room and shoot the third guard through the bars between rooms.

The switch (12) on the wall in the first room, near the doorway to the second room, controls the gate (13) behind the wall. Activating the switch opens the gate and allows a guard to enter the area. Shoot him through the nearby window. Two more guards take cover behind glass partitions (14) in this newly opened hallway/stairwell.

SECONDARY MISSION OBJECTIVE: OBTAIN THE INTERROGATION RECORDING

Find the reel-to-reel tape player in the second room (15) inside the security control room. Use your smart phone to record the audio from the machine. Make sure you stand close enough to get the audio icon on your phone before pressing the required record button. This completes this secondary mission.

The second switch (17) in the control room opens the remaining gate (18) on the right side of the security area. This, too, lets a guard into the hallways. Shoot him through the control room glass. When you progress up to the next stairwell (19), notice the four guards lined up near fire extinguishers on either side. Shoot the extinguishers. The spray blinds the guards and allows you to gun them all down with out much effort.

GRAB THE GRENADE LAUNCHER!
Make sure to visit the back room (16) to find a weapon crate housing a **grenade launching assault rifle**.

ARMORY

Move up to the locked gate (20) at the top of the stairs. Shoot through the bars to hit the guards inside the armory. Unlock the door using the switch on the left side of the door.

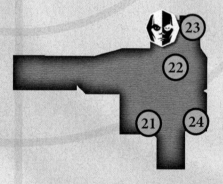

Clear the main room and then move to the right room. Take down any remaining soldiers. Shoot the propane tank (21) in the fenced in area from a room away. Watch the explosion blow a hole through the wall. Eliminate the enemies that appear around the hole. This is another way through the armory without having to pass through the metal detectors (22).

In the gate control room (**23**) you find a switch near the window that unlocks the gate outside. This gate closes whenever you trigger the metal detector with your weapons. So if this gate is closed, open it with this switch and crawl out the window or blow a hole in the wall with the propane tank (**21**) and go around this little trap. Also find **submachine guns** in the locked weapon locker and **Armor** on the counter along the back wall.

When you reach the stairwell (**24**), look up to the top level before climbing the stairs. Spot the guard and shoot him down from the staircase.

FOUR PILLAR ROOM

At the top of the stairs you find a weapon crate under a corner window. Another window in this nook gives you a view of the next hallway you need to enter (**25**). Shoot the servers at the end of the hallway. Enter the hallway and gun down the soldier that enters the hallway from the pillar room (**26**).

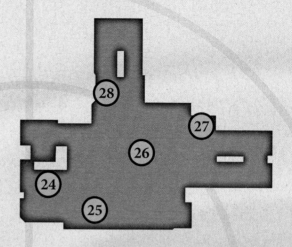

Fire on the room full of enemies through the hallway window. This allows you to control your exposure to the enemy by dropping below the window or heading back away from the window. Once you enter the pillar room, another three enemies also enter the room (all along the back wall in various locations). Gun them down and collect their weapons.

There are two open doorways that lead away from this room. Both pathways lead to the same area: the Server Room.

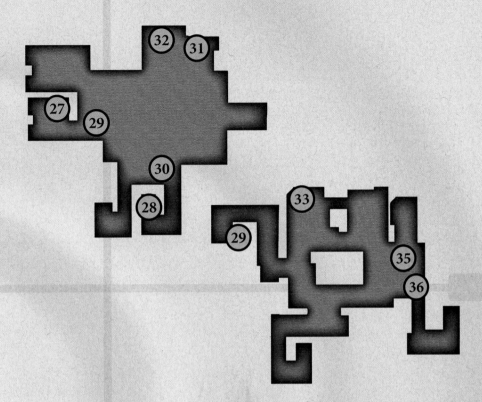

When you come up the stairs **(27)** or **(28)**, shoot into the server room sporadically to blow up the servers, taking out nearby enemies. Target and kill the enemies on the upper balcony. Continue up the stairs **(29)** or **(30)** depending on which route you took. Shoot any servers you see. You must shoot them all to complete the secondary mission.

On the top level of the server room, continue shooting any solider that appears around the balcony or remaining below in the server courtyard.

WALKTHROUGH

SECONDARY MISSION OBJECTIVE: DESTROY THE SERVERS

To get all the servers you must explore the hallways that lead to the server room to take out stand-alone units as well as destroy all the servers in the main server room.

There's a room (32) only accessible by traveling through a high ventilation shaft (31). This shaft is found in a nook on the first floor above a filing cabinet. Use this shaft to reach the room and destroy all the servers inside. Once you are done in this room you can leave by opening the now unlocked door.

SECONDARY MISSION OBJECTIVE: GATHER RUSSIAN INTELLIGENCE FOR MI6

Enter the office (33) on the top balcony level. Push the shiny filing cabinet on the right wall away from the hidden ventilation shaft. Bash the indicated buttons to move the furniture. This vent leads to a room with a secondary objective.

In the red-lit room (34) use your smartphone to hack and download Janus data from Mishkin's laptop on the desk. Raid the weapon locker in this room before you leave (back the way you came).

Head to the opposite end (35) of the server room balcony and defeat the two guards that appear. Follow the radar blip through a guarded room with stairwell access (36). Take the stairs down through a hallway and into Archive Hall.

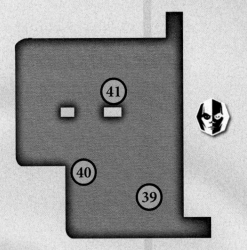

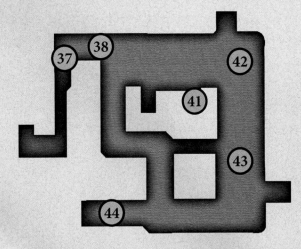

ENGINE ROOM

At the top of the stairs you reach a short hallway with no unlocked doors. At the end of the hallway is the open engine room (**30**). If you have them, use silenced weapons to keep reinforcements from entering this engine room battle. Start by subduing the nearest guard overlooking the engine pit. You can see more guards beyond the pit on the opposite end of this large room. Shoot the men you can see there now and then start moving down the left corridor to prevent any enemies from coming up behind you. Use the consoles for cover as you take on the many elite soldiers in this area.

ARCHIVE HALL

Within the corridor (**37**) after leaving the server room, Bond receives a call from Tanner on his smartphone. A helicopter passes the nearby windows. It's getting ready to drop elite enemies into the facility via zipline. Continue through the breach doorway ahead (**38**).

Gun down the three gunmen in front of you through the breach door. Head to the right end of the pathway, shoot the guard in the nook and check out the weapon chest with a **gun** and **Armor** near the cabinet in the corner. Don't forget to check out the weapon locker in this nook as well. Shoot the gunman on the first floor behind the counter by shooting over the balcony rail. When you head down the stairs, another guard rushes behind the counter. Shoot him before he achieves cover.

Follow the hallway and shoot the elite soldier that ziplines through the window. Around the corner, the soldiers drop smoke bombs to help cover their breach. Use the bookcases for cover (as they do) and begin picking off enemies one at a time as you slowly make your way around the room. Expect window breaches around each corner. Keep your weapon stock fresh using the weapons the enemies drop.

JANUS SYMBOL #30

You can see this Janus symbol outside the windows of the Archive Hall when you first encounter the elite window-breaching soldiers. The symbol is on the base of a distant statue. Shoot it through the window.

When you reach the last corner **(39),** before you get a view of the open middle area, you encounter multiple elite soldiers advancing and some set up in defensive positions in the distance, waiting for you. Use the hallway corner for cover as you first gun down those that rush toward you and then use the corner for cover as you pick off the remaining soldiers in the middle of the room, starting with the shooters on the upper level.

SECONDARY MISSION OBJECTIVE: GATHER RUSSIAN INTELLIGENCE FOR MI6

After clearing the middle area of enemies, move to the opposite hallway (40) to find the microfiche machine. Activate it and then use the smartphone to take a picture of the satellite image. Also find Armor and a weapon in the locked weapon chest nearby.

Use the stairs (41) to reach the top level and work your way around the room in a clockwise fashion. Expect heavier than normal resistance as the elite soldiers continue to zipline through the windows, starting with the first corner (42) at the top of the stairs.

At the end of the top floor you can either cross the bridge (43) or clamber over overturned bookshelves to make it to the exit in the back corner (44). Expect two soldiers to attack from this corner. One comes out of the exit and another smashes through the nearby window.

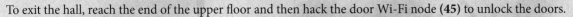

To exit the hall, reach the end of the upper floor and then hack the door Wi-Fi node (45) to unlock the doors.

BALCONY BATTLE ARENA

You enter this chamber via the second floor balcony. You see Ourumov and Natalya entering a lift on the lower floor, the doors closing behind them. Your goal is to call the lift using the switch (45) beside it while holding off attacking enemies and waiting for the lift to arrive. A wave of enemies spawn but no more appear until you have pressed the call button. Once this is done, a steady wave of four to five enemies attack while you wait for the lift.

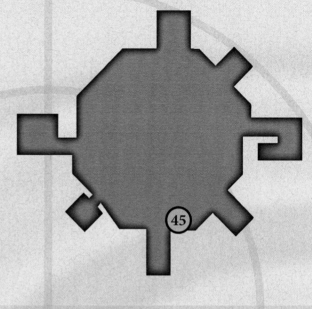

Use the landing on the stairwells to survive attacks that occur simultaneously on both floors. The stairs also draw enemies trying to reach the level you are on, so the enemy comes to you. Since your back is to a corner wall, the enemy can't sneak up on you. You can also vault over the upper balconies to the lower floor for a quick escape from pursuing enemies.

WATCH YOUR RADAR

Keep in mind that the red enemy icons with arrows are on a different level than you and those with no arrows are on the same level.

Use the **Armor** in the weapon crate at the bottom of one of the stairwells only when it is critical to survival. Don't waste it by taking it when you still have some armor remaining. Press the call button. Defeat the enemies and wait for the lift to open. Enter the lift as soon as it opens. Once on the lift, press the switch inside to reach the bunker.

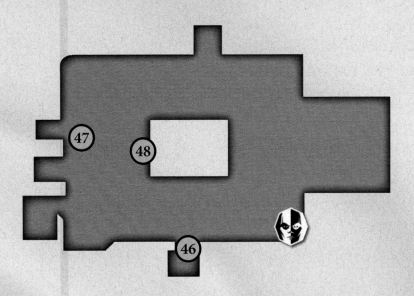

BUNKER

You enter the bunker area through a doorway **(46)** at the top of a staircase. The bunker is full of soldiers, so it's a good idea to start the battle with a silenced weapon to keep the initial chaos down. Crouch down and descend the stairs slowly. Take down the first soldier that comes into view and continue to sweep across the room, eliminating soldiers as they enter your view beyond the stairway cover.

The staircase has destructible cover that won't last long under heavy gunfire. Once the enemy is on high alert and is shooting from multiple directions, switch to your most powerful, long-range assault rifle (silenced or not). Also be on the lookout for thrown grenades. Target explosive containers near groups of enemies for maximum carnage.

The area contains plenty of destructive crates that can be used as cover. The control room (**47**) overlooks the bunker. Shoot the enemies in the control room through the observation window. Reaching this control room is your goal. Activating the controls in this location results in a prototype tank rising up on a floor lift.

JANUS SYMBOL #31
The last Janus symbol in this mission is behind a stack of crates positioned near the bottom of the entry staircase.

Use the staircase on the opposite side of the bunker to reach the second level control room (**47**). Gun down the reinforcing enemies inside.

SECONDARY MISSION OBJECTIVE: GATHER RUSSIAN INTELLIGENCE FOR MI6

At the far end of the control room, near the stairs, is a holograph machine with the blueprints of the secret tank. Activate the machine and then take a picture of the blueprint above the holographic image of the tank to complete this secondary objective.

Activate the switch on the console near the gap in the computers. Here you can get a clear view out the observation window to see the tank being lifted into the room through a shaft in the floor.

Remain in the control room to stage your attack on the many waves of soldiers that appear after the tank is revealed. Watch both stairwell entrances into the control room so no one sneaks up behind you. Try to take down as many of the soldiers as you can the moment they appear out in the garage area. If they move out of your view underneath the control tower, then move to the stairwell to thwart an ambush.

When you've eliminated all the enemies, approach the front of the tank (48) and press the indicated button to get inside. Bond blows a hole in the bunker wall and drives the tank out.

TANK

PURSUE OURUMOV

FREEWAY COLLAPSE

Some thirty minutes or so after stealing the Prototype Tank from the bunker beneath the Military Archives we pick up the action with Bond pursuing Ourumov's Humvee through the outskirts of St. Petersburg. As Ourumov races down the newly built highway ahead of Bond, a helicopter attempts to intercept the tank by destroying the road in front of Bond. Now that the highway isn't an option, Tanner plots a course for Bond to catch up with, and attempt to apprehend, Ourumov and rescue Natalya.

You begin the tank (**1**) adventure in a pile of rubble under the collapsed overpass. You must pursue Ourumov without letting him get too far away in order to complete this time-limited mission.

SECONDARY MISSIONS & JANUS SYMBOLS

There are no secondary missions or Janus symbols to collect during the tank challenge. Just drive, shoot and survive to get to the train in time to complete this mission.

You are introduced to basic tank controls: movement and aiming. As you progress across the building site towards the first objective marker, smash through barriers and drive over most any object. Shoot the rocket-launching soldier on the balcony above the hotel carport (**2**).

HOTEL

Pass through the carport and use a lock-on missile on the helicopter in the next area. Use the lock-on missiles on just about any vehicle or helicopter you can. This saves you time by eliminating the need to manually aim missiles at moving targets while driving as fast as you can to keep up with Ourumov. Destroy the vehicles in the following pit (3) and veer left up the incline. Continue achieving missile lock on the ground vehicles.

THE PITS

At the second pit (4) you face multiple vehicles and helicopters. Don't stop to shoot. Target and shoot as you drive through the pit and up the inclined road (5) to the left around the round building. Aim for explosive objects to help take out multiple enemies with one attack. Look for fuel trucks and suspended pipes to manually target.

CITY STREET

Shoot the tanker (6) near the narrow street (7) and buildings you first reach. Doing so takes out some approaching Humvees. Follow the street and use guided missiles on the helicopter and more Humvees coming right at you.

ONRAMP

Beyond the narrow business street you spot a collapsing building in your path (8). The tower leans up against an adjacent building creating a tunnel through. Follow the tunnel to the onramp (9).

155

Take out the military vehicles and helicopters along the circular onramp to keep them from whittling down your defenses.

FREEWAY

At the top of the ramp, where it meets the freeway, jet fighters try attacking you. They miss, but take out sections **(10)** of the freeway you must steer around. Drive over the rubble that looks like a roadblock **(11)**.

Just beyond the barricade you drive over, you seem to have Ourumov in your sights. Before you know it a large explosion disintegrates the entire freeway. You instantly find yourself off-road **(12)** below the freeway.

TUNNEL

Use guided missiles on the many helicopters in the pit before the tunnel **(13)**. The tunnel is large enough to accommodate the choppers, so expect resistance inside as well.

COLLAPSED BUILDING TUNNEL

Just out of the tunnel you reach a parking lot. The building on the other side of the parking lot collapses under a huge explosion. However, a small tunnel remains at its base. Steer your tank into this hole (14) before taking too much more damage from helicopter attacks. Drive through the tunnel and run over the many cars in the exit parking lot.

ATTACK HELICOPTER

As you exit the building parking lot you come face-to-face with the largest attack helicopter yet (15). It takes three to four guided missiles to stop this beast. Keep driving to beat the time limit, but target and shoot this chopper every chance you get, so it doesn't take you out in the home stretch.

As you gun it for the last tunnel (16) that marks the end of the challenge, you confront multiple helicopter attacks while military vehicles move in place to stop you from reaching your goal. Use non-stop guided missile attacks while concentrating on steering directly into the tunnel to end the mission.

PRIMARY OBJECTIVES

Enter the Train

Rescue Natalya.

Escape the Train.

BOARD THE TRAIN

Having pursued Ourumov's Humvee through the construction site of a modern business park, Bond arrives at the partially constructed railway station just in time to see Natalya being escorted aboard a departing postal train. The train begins to depart and Bond must stop it and rescue Natalya. Still in the tank, Bond moves alongside the train, ramming into it.

Eventually, at the head of the train, Bond forces the engine car away from the rest of the train, derailing most of the forward carriages. Exiting the tank you notice a direct route to the train is blocked by wreckage; you must enter the half constructed station on foot and find a way onto the train.

Begin the battle by taking cover behind the nearby crates (1) and shooting the enemies that show themselves in the next area ahead. Expect five enemies in this area before pushing through the occupied room (2). Pick up the dropped weapons (**Vargen FH-7 with Reflex Sight**), head through the objective marker and continue through the structure.

Just past the objective marker you reach a set of escalators (3) with an open room to the left. Shoot the enemy that advances and then cautiously investigate the opening on the right. Use the escalator side of the opening for cover as you shoot the enemies in the open construction site (4). Expect another seven enemies to battle. A couple of enemies make their way down the escalators to attack, so keep your eye on the radar.

You can choose to take the escalators up and attack from high or you can hoof it through the construction site and use the various objects for cover while battling the enemy. As you make your way toward the next objective marker **(5)** expect another squad of enemies to appear. You also spot a helicopter hovering around. The helicopter poses no threat so keep your focus on the gunman and not getting surrounded.

USE THE BARRELS

Look for explosive barrels to target. They not only take out nearby enemies but some of them can start a chain of destruction that takes out even greater numbers.

Climb the metal grate ramps to the objective marker **(5)** and find the **Armor** on the wire spool.

Just beyond this platform is a large open construction area **(6)** filled with gunmen on many different levels. Take cover behind the objects where the Armor is located. Shoot the fuel barrel on the crane-suspended girder. This causes it to drop on the enemies below it. Look for explosive barrels near many enemy positions. Shoot the barrels to take out multiple enemies at once.

JANUS SYMBOL #32

Before you leave the platform where you found the Armor (5), turn and look up to the sky and find the crane above your head to the right. Now follow it down to a scaffolding wall. Shoot the Janus symbol found on billboard art in between the plywood walls.

If you follow the hallway **(7)** under the Janus symbol to the end, you find yourself on a high scaffold overlooking another section of the construction site **(8)** filled with more gunmen. Use the height advantage this angle provides and attack from here first, then return to the ground level to proceed.

Continue the assault on the gunmen on the various levels of construction ahead. Vault over the edge of the scaffold to reach the lower platform with the large spool. Focus some firepower on the rocket-launching enemy on the high platform in the distance.

Make your way down to the ground level and begin attacking the gunmen around the left corner **(9)** near and beyond a parked forklift. If you head up the nearby ramp, before the corner, you can get the jump on a lot of the enemies that try to rush your position. They try to climb a platform across from yours, turning their backs to you, making them extremely vulnerable to your fire.

Infiltrate the next area **(10)** using the large machinery and other objects for cover as you target gunmen and explosive materials. Follow the ramp to the upper level in this area. This ramp system leads to the cab of a large crane **(11)**.

Pull the lever in the crane cab to drop a large concrete pipe onto the train below. This creates a large explosion, instantly wiping out a handful of enemies.

Now use the catwalks around the crane to move about the train area, picking off enemies from behind cover below.

JANUS SYMBOL #33

As you leave the crane cab (11) *after dropping the pipe on the train, move down the first ramp and notice the gap in the platform where another ramp would take you down to the ground level (if there were another ramp). Drop down into this crevice and look at the side of the blue, canvas-covered crates to find the Janus symbol stuck to the side of the platform in the dark corner.*

When you reach the burning train section where you dropped the large pipe (12), expect resistance ahead as you follow the objective marker. The enemies run out of a pipe and take cover behind crate stacks. Gun them down before they can cause much trouble.

WALKTHROUGH

Clear the area and the down ramp **(13)** between the pipes and the parked train. Follow the ramp to the bottom. Defeat the gunman there and then prepare to gun down two more at the far end of a large drainage pipe that you use as a tunnel to reach the other side of the large concrete wall **(14)**.

At the top of the ramp out of the pipe tunnel, reload and prepare to fight three enemies to your extreme left. Climb the slope slowly to get a bead on your enemies before they see you. Two men run along the top of the train while the most threatening target stands near the edge of your slope **(15)**.

THE TRAIN

At the top of your slope **(15)**, look left for the not-so-damaged train doorway. Bash the indicated buttons to pry the twisted door open so you can get inside the train.

Once on the train, have your favorite weapon ready to shoot the enemies coming at you from the next car ahead. Use the provided cover for safety but try to take out the gunmen before they find good cover.

The doors to the second car are automatic and open when you near them. The next car is already full of gunmen who have already found adequate cover. Remain on the original car using the door for cover while taking out the nearest gunmen first. Push into that car when it is safe to do so.

As you make your way through the second car, keep your attention to the right side of the train. When you see windows, look for the enemy gunmen outside. There is an explosive barrel between the first two that shakes things up a bit. Shoot them through the windows.

JANUS

JANUS SYMBOL #34

Before you leave the train, look back out the window where you staged your last battle. You spot this Janus symbol on the back of a scaffold wall, toward the back of the train.

Vault over the small rail in the train to reach the exit (**17**). Bond pries the doors open and walks into a little party at the back of the train.

Bond comes face to face with Ourumov and Onatopp. They are surprised to see him. Natalya is immediately held at gunpoint while two other Janus soldiers raise their guns towards Bond. Ourumov is killed by Onatopp who then escapes with the GoldenEye control device.

The moment that she escapes, time slows and you are able to take out the three Janus soldiers before they can react. As Bond helps Natalya up, Onatopp returns and throws a grenade into the carriage before escaping again.

Bond throws Natalya into the far corner of the carriage and shields her from the grenade. When control returns to you, notice some of the carpet of the carriage has been destroyed revealing a maintenance hatch underneath.

Smoke is beginning to fill the carriage. You need to shoot each of the latches off the hatch so both you and Natalya can escape from the burning train. Once recovered, Natalya tells Bond that Ourumov was headed for the Statue Park in St. Petersburg.

MEMORIAL PARK

PRIMARY OBJECTIVES

Investigate Statue Park

Gather Photographic Evidence

Investigate the Janus Presence

Escape the Prototype Helicopter

SECONDARY OBJECTIVES

Obtain Intel on Janus Technology (3)

Record the Encrypted Transmission

INVESTIGATE STATUE PARK

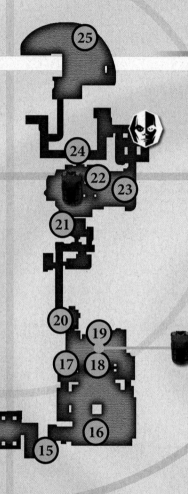

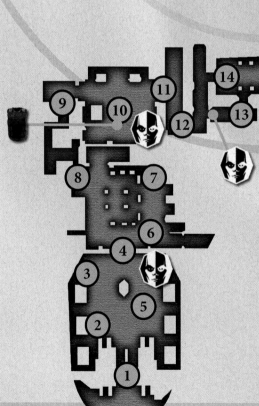

STATUE PARK

Having saved Natalya from the burning train, Bond and Natalya make their way to investigate Memorial Park. Bond leaves Natalya with the car and a gun for protection.

Inside the covered park entrance **(1)** you can spot a single guard patrolling the stairs just beyond the exit of your building. Quickly shoot him with three or four silenced shots. Take his weapon.

Find the broken area in the concrete balcony rail **(2)** and drop down to the lower left area of the statue park. Notice the guards along this pathway. Crouch down and walk behind the planters on the left to come up behind the furthest guard **(3)** on this walkway with his back to you. He stands facing the large, overturned statue head. Subdue him and take his weapon.

This leaves three guards near the exit **(4)** and three back the way you came, but on the right side of the park. Return towards the entrance of the park and silently shoot the one guard that patrols away from the other two **(5)**. Sneak up on the two guards gathered around a barrel fire and shoot them both very quickly with silenced rounds so the second one shot does not have time to raise an alert. If you pop the first one in the head, only one shot is required to kill him, then quickly auto-aim and shoot the second gunman.

Now that you have the entire park cleared except for the few enemies beyond the cars near the entrance, you can afford to make a little noise. Shoot the remaining guards, using vehicle explosions to eliminate enemies using them for cover. All the commotion brings two additional enemies from further ahead. Gun them down and then take down the two guards in the connecting alleyway **(6)** that don't leave their post.

JANUS SYMBOL #35

Before leaving the park for the connecting alleyway, look at the back neck area of the statue to the right of the park exit. This corner statue holds the first Janus symbol in this level.

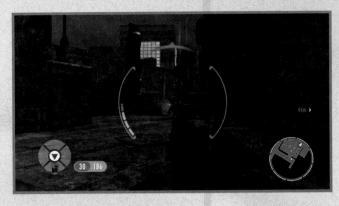

Beyond the alley is a left turn in the path where you must pass through a tank memorial. There are no enemies in this area. At the end of this path is the entrance to another large park about the size of the first one you cleared. Remain at the entrance, taking cover behind the right column, and start shooting everyone in sight. Most of the enemies seek you out and you can simply gun them down as they funnel toward you. They never arrive more than two at a time, so you won't get overpowered.

STORM DRAIN

Once the area is clear as far as you can see from your position, move in and head to the back where you find the entrance to a tunnel. Gun down the guards that hold a position near the entrance. Enter this tunnel (8).

But before you leave, there's a secondary objective you can take care of in this room. Follow the tunnel to a small set of stairs. Below you see a sewer system. Follow this sewer tunnel to the end and climb the ladder to exit (9) into another area of the park that houses a small guard building.

GUARD STATION

Take cover behind a column near the sewer exit and begin shooting the many guards on the road ahead. Keep your eye on the radar—an enemy is often posted to your extreme left within all the planters, which make great cover. Once you have cleared many of the enemies, shoot the sniper on top of the guard station (10) and then climb the ladder to reach the guard station rooftop.

EXPLOSIONS ARE EFFICIENT

Shooting the vehicle as it pulls up is a good way to take out an entire group of enemies at once.

After climbing up onto the station rooftop **(10)**, shoot the rightmost skylight and drop down into the building below.

Inside the backroom you dropped into is a weapon chest. Shoot it open and take the **Armor** and the **Ivana Spec-R + Silencer,** if you wish. You can use the door in the room to reach the outside again. But before you leave, there's a secondary objective you can take care of in this room. To enter the main room in the guard station, you do not need to drop through a skylight, you can simply go through the open front doors. In the back cell is a weapon chest containing an **Ivana Spec-R** without a silencer.

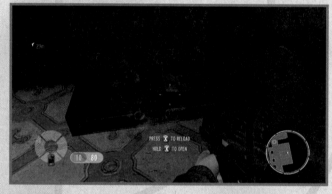

SECONDARY MISSION OBJECTIVE: OBTAIN INTEL ON JANUS TECHNOLOGY (1/3)

Access the locked back room in the guardhouse by dropping in through the skylight on the rooftop. Open the green drone gun crate and then step back and take a picture with your smartphone.

Notice there are two shortcut sewer tunnel access points in this area. One ground entry ladder is found on the left, planter isle side of the park and the other entrance is on the ground to the right of the exit area (11). A weapon chest is located near the exit ladder.

JANUS SYMBOL #36
Before leaving the guard station area, look to the right corner near the exit (11) for the Janus symbol up high in an architectural archway.

Exit the guard station area and you reach a closed gate (12). Bash the indicated buttons to pry the gate open. Just through the gate is a lower park with two entrances. Take the entrance straight ahead from the gate you pried open or you expose yourself to many more enemies at once when using the second park entrance that leads to a high balcony.

JANUS SYMBOL #37
After prying open the gate, head straight across the street and pass under the archway and stop. Look behind you and up to the top of the arch. Here you find the third Janus symbol in this level. Shoot it.

Continue through the narrow passage beyond the Janus Symbol #37 and stop beside a column on the right (13) that gives you an angled view into the park on your left. Shoot the enemies that appear in your line of sight into the park. Continue to shoot anyone that enters this view. If no more guards appear for a while, but you can still see live targets on the radar, move back to the previous street and attack from the balcony entrance (14).

Enter the park and pick up dropped weapons. Through the exit **(15)** you find a rubble-covered path. Find the small hole in the wall to get around the rubble and into the park.

GATHER PHOTOGRAPHIC EVIDENCE
MEMORIAL PARK

When you enter the memorial park, you are prompted to answer your smartphone. You convey to MI6 that this seems to be a staging area and that you'll be sending back pictures. Notice the many enemies in the park by looking at your radar. There are two snipers on rooftops in the area and many armed gunmen around the park. You can stealthily clear this entire area by using a nearby sniper rifle.

Crouch walk down the hill on which you start and work your way to the extreme right area where you find a covered walkway. Wait for the patrolling guard in this area to walk with his back to you through this covered area. Shoot him with a silenced weapon. Pick up the **CP-208** sniper rifle with silencer leaning up against the railing in this covered walkway **(16)**.

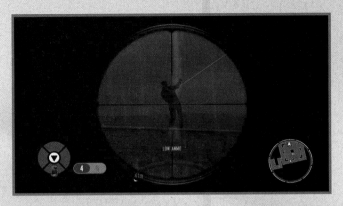

Use the rifle to shoot the two snipers on the rooftops. One is on the right side of the park and the other is on the opposite end above the exit **(18)**.

Use the sniper rifle to shoot all the distant enemies near the exit and save the nearest two gathered around the fire barrel for last. Use your silenced P99 to take them out quickly, one after the other.

Avoid the laser site of the autogun near the exit and use your smartphone on the laptop **(17)** on the railing near the gun to change the gun's loyalty to your side. Using this weapon during a non-stealthy attack is a good idea. It clears the enemy from the park if you can make it to it without getting killed.

Shoot the green-lit security cams from above the exit **(18)** and enter the building.

SECURE THE ROOM
UNDERGROUND TUNNELS

As you enter the tunnels, find the door switch straight ahead on the wall **(19)**. Activate this lockdown switch. This locks the exterior doors, keeping any potential reinforcements from entering. The interior doors to the left are unlocked and you can hear guards on the other side, but nothing happens…yet.

Find the laptop on the weapon crates in the middle of the room. Take a picture of the laptop screen to complete the current objective. These are details of the flight plans to Africa. In the security monitor, Bond spots Natalya getting captured, but he must stick with the mission and deal with that later.

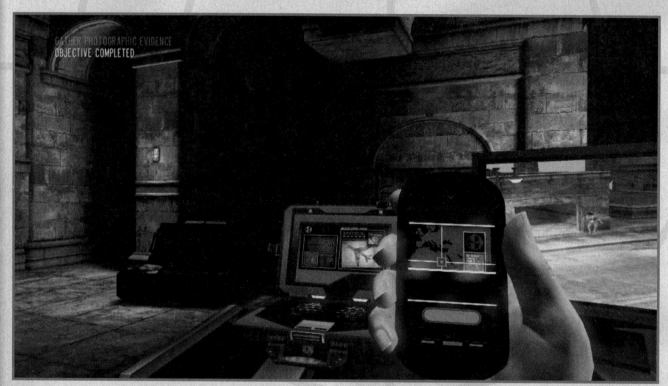

INVESTIGATE THE JANUS PRESENCE

As soon as control returns to you after completing the photographic evidence objective, the guards open the double doors and begin a serious attack. Start shooting as soon as the doors open. Back up into the small room in the back or they begin to overpower you. A second wave occurs after you clear the first handful of enemies. Two guards remain at a post in the next hallway. Go ahead and eliminate them and then return to the first room. Find the **Armor** and the **Ivana Spec-R** in the open weapon chest on the floor.

When you exit the initial tunnel room you find a small room to the left and the continuing route on the right. Use your smartphone to take a picture of the weapon crates behind the bars in the cell on your left. You can take any of the weapons you want through the cell bars.

DRAINAGE TUNNELS

Head through the next set of double doors (**20**) and pick up the **Night Vision Goggles** from the open weapon case on the floor. Turn on the night vision by pressing up on the D-pad. Reload your assault rifles and then head down the tunnel stairs and prepare for a big shootout in the drainage tunnels. Use the barrels on the left for cover as you pop up and shoot the many elite soldiers that attack.

Work your way through the tunnels eliminating the many elite guards by using the small maze to your advantage. Attack the enemy through one doorway and then rush to another to attack from another angle to keep them confused.

PACKAGING CHAMBER

Push through the exit double doors (**21**) to enter a very short hallway with another set of double doors ahead of you. Through these doors is a large staging room with many enemies working on packaging servers and others just patrolling and watching the area. To complete the secondary mission "Record the Encrypted Transmission" you must take them all out stealthily, as to not raise an alarm.

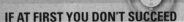

IF AT FIRST YOU DON'T SUCCEED
As soon as the alarm is sounded (when you are spotted or heard), you fail the objective. You can restart at the previous checkpoint if you want to try it again.

WALKTHROUGH

SECONDARY MISSION OBJECTIVE: RECORD THE ENCRYPTED TRANSMISSION

Begin stealthily clearing the shipping room by silently shooting the man with his back to you just beyond the entry balcony. If you perform an auto aim, manually aim a bit higher for the head. A single headshot takes the enemies out with one bullet and reduces the possibility of being heard.

Move left and shoot the man with his back to you in the corner. From the same position, pivot and shoot the man on the landing, facing the next hallway.

While you're still on the entry balcony, strafe back near the entrance and shoot the guard that moves from a server crate back to a laptop for data entry. Shoot him when his back is to you.

Drop off the edge of the balcony near where you entered the room and take the Armor from the table. You start receiving smartphone warnings that there is audio to record nearby. While you are here you can take care of the secondary objective: Obtain intel on Janus technology (2/3). Afterward, reload your silent weapon and strafe around the large crates beyond the armor to reveal the two guards working together on sealing a crate. Shoot one in the head and then quickly put enough bullets in the body of the second one so he can't raise an alarm.

Now head to the right side of the room and to the right corner balcony. Wait on the floor looking through the rails, waiting for the patrolling guard to come into view in the hallway ahead. Fill him full of silenced rounds. From here you begin to hear your main target speaking, but you can't record from this far away.

Move to the left front corner of the small balcony (22) with the last two guards. This is the hardest part and similar to the two guards you took out while they were packing the crate earlier. Shoot one guard in the head and then quickly auto aim and fill the second guard full of silenced bullets as fast as you can to avoid the alarm.

Crouch walk up into the next hallway and sneak up behind the man on the phone with his back to you in the control room. Pull out the smartphone and keep approaching him until you get a green light to record his conversation. Afterward, dispatch him.

SECONDARY MISSION OBJECTIVE: OBTAIN INTEL ON JANUS TECHNOLOGY (1/3)

Access the locked back room in the guardhouse by dropping in through the skylight on the rooftop. Open the green drone gun crate and then step back and take a picture with your smartphone.

DRAINAGE TUNNELS

Exit the control room through the hole in the back wall that leads down to the drainage tunnels (**23**). Turn on your night vision goggles and eliminate the elite soldiers in these tunnels.

JANUS SYMBOL #38

The last Janus symbol in this level is located in this drainage tunnel. Find the locked gate which marks a dead-end. Look through the bars and down the next hallway to find the Janus symbol stuck on the side of the brick wall. Shoot it through the bars.

Continue following the drain through a number of elite soldier posts. In the long straightaway (**24**) expect two elite soldiers to zipline down into the tunnel through a couple of windows above. Find the stairs that lead out of the tunnels and to an open gate where you can see the parked prototype helicopter (**25**).

PROTOTYPE HELICOPTER

When you pass through the gate, sniper laser sights train on Bond and a surprising foe reappears. Bond is shot with a tranquilizer or is knocked over the head from behind. Either way, he ends up tied up inside the driver's seat of the prototype helicopter.

ESCAPE THE PROTOTYPE HELICOPTER

When Bond comes to, he looks around the instrument panel, sees his hands tied to the flight stick and that two guided missiles have been launched from the helicopter and are making their way through the air back to the helicopter. As soon as control returns to you, look to your hard left and place the dot reticle on the "Break Glass" sign over the ejection seat button. Bond smashes the glass with his head and activates the ejection seat.

MISSION 6: NIGERIA

JUNGLE

CLEAN ENERGY FACILITY, NORTHWEST NIGERIA

PRIMARY OBJECTIVES

Locate the Pan-African Power Solar Plant

Neutralize Xenia Onatopp

SECONDARY OBJECTIVES

Disable the Drone Guns (Agent Mode and above)

Destroy the Ammunition Caches (007 Classic Mode)

LOCATE THE PAN-AFRICAN POWER SOLAR PLANT

CRASH SITE

Bond has acquired the coordinates of a complex possibly housing the second GoldenEye satellite dish. As he gets near these coordinates his plane is shot down somewhere in the jungle.

In the meantime, several Janus squads have been sent to locate the plane wreck in order to confirm that there are no survivors. As Bond recovers from the crash he finds himself next to his burning airplane. You hear helicopters as Tanner warns Bond to get away from there. A squad is abseiling down from a helicopter and they're moving towards his position **(1)**.

After the troops move into position around the crash site sneak up and subdue the lone soldier closest to you, but the next two soldiers remain too close to each other.

There's no reason to remain stealthy here. Take the first enemy's shotgun, **Drumhead Type-12**, reload it and use it on the second two soldiers. The gunshots alert more guards further ahead and they file up the hill (2) to attack. Remain near the crash site and just pick them off one at a time as they show themselves.

When no more soldiers seek you out on the hill, head down the slope and move slowly through the clearing (3). More soldiers move toward you from further ahead. Gun them down before they shoot.

Follow the narrow jungle path ahead to the next objective marker (4). Vault over the large log to continue. Once you're over the log, more enemies begin to appear on the radar. Quickly shoot the two visible soldiers with their backs to you, one after the other, to remain stealthy. The third soldier in the area can be spotted to the right of a large boulder on the right in the clearing. Gun him down and take the dropped weapons.

Use the rock (**5**) that the soldier was beside for cover while you shoot the next group of soldiers in the distance (**6**).

SECONDARY MISSION OBJECTIVE: DISABLE THE DRONE GUNS (1/9)

As you reach the first bend in the path with a mountain's edge view of the jungle valley you find a drone gun. Just before you reach the gun you can find a laptop controller on the left side of the path. Hack this terminal. This is the first of 9 drone guns you need to disable to complete this objective.

184

In the next clearing (**7**) you spot many enemies on the radar. You can silently shoot the soldier in clear view to your left (**8**). Take him down quickly to remain stealthy for a while longer.

Head to where his body dropped (**8**) and you find two more nearby soldiers in a lower pathway. Instead of shooting them, try getting close enough to the edge of the rock cover on the ledge above them to hack the drone gun. This eliminates them and the many soldiers further ahead you can't even see yet.

WHEN STEALTH DOESN'T WORK OUT...

If you make noise, many soldiers attack via that lower path from the left and as it bends away in a hairpin turn to the right. Watch both sides and gun down anyone that appears.

SECONDARY MISSION OBJECTIVE: DISABLE THE DRONE GUNS (2/9)

Make this gun work for you during nearby battles by activating this drone gun early on. Hack the laptop with your smartphone. This gun is placed up on a hill to your left and annihilates a team of enemies further ahead.

SECONDARY MISSION OBJECTIVE: DISABLE THE DRONE GUNS (3/9)

This laptop control system is located not far from the last one. On the left side of the trail, avoid the purple laser searching for enemies and then find and hack this laptop to make the drone gun your friend.

You follow the forest path for a while without any drone guns or enemies to be found. When you begin to hear voices, slow down and crouch walk. At a fork **(9)** in the path you find a soldier **(10)** standing guard with his back to you. It's hard to tell this is a fork, but the upper pathway on the left **(11)** is through the foliage. Silently shoot the soldier.

A patrolling guard walks towards your victim so make sure to take the first one out while the other is not around. If they are too close together you must be prepared to gun down the second one very quickly. If you wish to start a gunfight here, it's not a bad place to do so. Wait at the fork and the enemy files in along the lower path (10) or you see them coming at you along the upper pathway (11). Either way, you have time to gun them down by the time they reach a range they are comfortable shooting from. Following the upper pathway for a short distance is a great way to get the advantage on the enemy on the lower path.

The upper pathway turns into a large, overturned tree, which forks near the end. Follow it to the end (12) to shoot enemies below and to find a sniper at the very end of the tree path, standing guard around the right cliff side.

SECONDARY MISSION OBJECTIVE: DISABLE THE DRONE GUNS (4/9)

The laptop for the next drone gun is located just beyond the upper tree pathway on the ground, on the left side of the pathway.

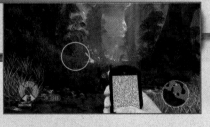

As you follow the continuing pathway, you come to a narrow, winding trail (13) where you can hear the sounds of helicopters flying overhead. Just a short way beyond this point you reach the waterfall area (14).

WATERFALL

The waterfall area is home to a large troop of soldiers and a couple of drone guns. You have to travel a particular way through the terrain to avoid being annihilated by the drone guns. Although you can easily shoot over the berm at the guards standing around a nearby tree, it's best to wait and shoot the soldier in the water moving up your path from the waterfall **(15)** and then double back up the path and shoot the soldiers appearing over the berm.

TWO BIRDS WITH ONE STONE

If you picked up the silenced sniper rifle and still carry it with you, you can have some fun lining up soldiers with nearby partners. Line their heads up and put one bullet through each of them. This is a great way to remain stealthy and save rounds. There are a couple soldiers in the distance near a distant drone gun that you can also take out this way from nearly the same position.

JANUS SYMBOL #39

*Follow the waterfall stream **(15)** around the first wide corner and look to your right as you move upstream. You find a small tunnel **(16)** under the road with an **Armor** in the middle. Continue through to the other side and you can find the Janus symbol behind the waterfall.*

With that fresh Armor on you can get by the first drone gun in the area without losing health (the Armor may be no good afterward, but you'll be alive). Start your sprint from the stream corner under the log bridge **(17)**. Here you have a clear view of the drone gun on top of the cave entrance. If you stand close enough to the rock here, you can turn that on from the stream and clear out many enemies effortlessly. Now follow the stream and run under the gun **(18)** and into the cave, avoiding the second gun's laser pointer. Before you run, shoot any enemies you see from this angle to make it easier on yourself once you are on the other side of the cave.

While in the cave, wait for any enemies to enter from the exit area. Gun them down and the exit the cave.

Sniping guards from a distance and pre-hacking the cave drone gun clears the caves of enemies. Follow the objective marker (19) out of the cave and around some small boulders.

SECONDARY MISSION OBJECTIVE: DISABLE THE DRONE GUNS (5/9)

You find this drone gun laptop on a weapon chest near the objective marker as you exit the cave to pass under a drone gun safely. Hack it with the smartphone.

SECONDARY MISSION OBJECTIVE: DISABLE THE DRONE GUNS (6/9)

From the fifth drone gun laptop, pivot around and look at the area above the cave you just passed through. Find the worn rock formations that look like ancient tiles. This ramp leads you to the top of the cave where you can find the sixth laptop that turns the cave-top drone gun to your side. This drone gun can also be hacked from the stream below when you first enter this area.

Follow the pathway (20) beside the sixth drone gun laptop on top of the cave. Shoot the two enemies along this pathway and notice the large, dead, hollow tree-bridge that sits above this pathway. You can access this bridge from a higher path (21) on the left. Take this path to find the next Janus symbol.

JANUS SYMBOL #40

As soon as you cross the hollow tree bridge (21), turn to the right and look at the nook between the edge of the log and the canyon side to find this Janus symbol.

At the end of the pathway **(22)** is a plateau near the back of the jungle Janus camp. A number of guards patrol the area. You can subdue the nearest guard gazing over the cliff's edge with his back to you. If you choose to subdue him, back up quickly after the deed to avoid the drone gun laser trying to track you. The drone gun is located on the control room **(24)** rooftop, around the corner.

There's one more patrolling guard on the cliff's edge further ahead. A silenced bullet is the best way to deal with him. As you round the corner to figure out what to do with the drone gun, you also spot three more soldiers. Gun them down quickly—they have no cover so you can eliminate them while taking little to no damage.

The shooting often attracts two other guards in the distant right corner, back near the pipes. Gun then down before they know there's even a fight. Hide behind the tower base **(23)** in the middle of the field and then watch the drone gun laser move across the yard. When it moves past you, run to the control room door heading along the left side of the tower for the most direct route.

SECONDARY MISSION OBJECTIVE: DISABLE THE DRONE GUNS (7/9)

From the back porch of the control room (24), hack the laptop on the weapon crates to the right of the stairs. The drone gun over your head cannot shoot at such a steep angle; you're safe here.

JANUS CAMP 1

Shoot the padlock from the backdoor of the control room and head inside **(24)**. You find a **Terralite III with ACOG Scope** in the front room. Exit the front door onto a catwalk overlooking a large, two-story military camp. Shoot the patrolling guard near the stairs.

SECONDARY MISSION OBJECTIVE: DESTROY THE AMMUNITION CACHES (1/3)

As you leave the initial control tower (24) you can find the first ammunition cache tucked in the back corner of the control tower and the camp's back wall. From a good distance, shoot the silver explosive barrels. You have a little delay to get further away if you need to before it explodes.

After shooting the first guard, head down the stairs (your only option unless you go across the pipe bridge). Wait at the bottom of the first flight of stairs **(25)**. Enemies start coming up one of the two staircases that reach the ground level ahead. This is a choke point. Stay here and mow down anyone that shows up. Keep an eye on your radar to make sure no one comes across the bridge behind you.

Now backtrack to the pipe bridge and clear any enemies that dare cross. With that done, peek over the edge of the bridge and eliminate all the enemies below, as well as all the reinforcements that come through the main gate (27).

JANUS SYMBOL #41

Head across the pipe bridge (26) and stop at the rail. Do not turn down the stairs. Stand looking at the end of the pipes where they meet the fort wall. You spot the shiny symbol behind a bush on the right side of the pipes.

SECONDARY MISSION OBJECTIVE: DESTROY THE AMMUNITION CACHES (2/3)

Follow the pipe bridge down to the opposite side of camp. Here you find a control room that houses explosives near ammunition. You can safely shoot the explosives while standing on the stairs across the road. Use a scoped weapon to hit your mark.

SECONDARY MISSION OBJECTIVE: DISABLE THE DRONE GUNS (8/9)

Find a drone gun and laptop in the control tower (28) near the back of the camp where the truck is parked. The gun and laptop are on the second floor. Hack the laptop inside.

SECONDARY MISSION OBJECTIVE: DISABLE THE DRONE GUNS (9/9)

The final drone gun laptop is located in the control room closest to the exit gate on the ground level. There's also a weapon locker to raid in there as well. Hack the laptop to complete the objective.

WALKTHROUGH

To leave the camp, head to the front gate (**27**) and hack the door lock node on the left side.

JANUS CAMP 2

Follow the road to a bricked path on the right side of the road. The main gate is locked. You must take this pathway. Climb down into the bunker entrance at the end of the path (**28**). This is a backdoor to another control tower. The front door is open to the next camp (**30**) where an attack helicopter is hovering and gunning for you.

Use the large construction pipe sections in the camp as cover as you run from one to the next to avoid the helicopter fire. Defeat the soldiers along the way. When you are out of pipes, run from log piles to the yellow construction vehicles.

JANUS SYMBOL #42

The final Janus symbol in this level is on the back side of the second construction crane. Shoot it after clearing the area of enemies and while continuing to avoid helicopter attacks.

Two trucks full of soldiers come screaming up and sliding sideways, unloading their occupants as quickly as possible in the bend in the road (31). Aim for the fuel tanks on the trucks to destroy the vehicles and hopefully most of the soldiers along with them.

BRIDGE

Use the burning truck chassis for cover from the soldiers and the attack helicopter near the bridge (33) and the last bunker (32). Pop up from cover to defeat the soldiers and then make a break for the bunker.

SECONDARY MISSION OBJECTIVE: DESTROY THE AMMUNITION CACHES (3/3)

The final ammunition cache is on the rooftop of the last bunker (32). Shoot the silver explosive barrel from a distant area behind cover. This includes any area from the crates outside the bunker across the road and as far back as the corner where the two trucks pulled up. Aim for the smidgen of silver tank you can see from these distances while avoiding the helicopter attack.

Once inside the bunker, swivel around and attack the reinforcements that arrive as soon as you enter the building. Shoot through the windows and the doorway.

TAKING OUT THE CHOPPER

Move along the bridge using every possible cover opportunity. You need to use all the crates for cover or you won't make it. Sprint from crate stack to crate stack, zigzagging across the bridge to get to the next nearest stack while avoiding the helicopter's missiles that are destroying large sections of the bridge.

From the final stack of crates on the left side of the bridge, sprint directly for the guided missile launcher **(34)** on the right and press the control button to fire a missile at the helicopter.

NEUTRALIZE XENIA ONATOPP

When you go to push the button on the SAM battery, Onatopp rappels from the helicopter above and attacks. To dominate in the hand-to-hand combat with Onatopp you must prepare to press the correct buttons that appear on screen within a reasonable amount of time.

After a few brutal blows with her left and right, she raises both hands to smash your face. Press the indicated button to block her and push her off in one move.

When Onatopp starts kicking, press the indicated button to block her leg. Repeat this button press again as she kicks with the other leg.

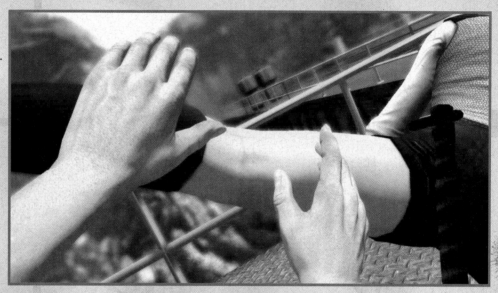

Press the Vault button to block her fist from hitting you in the face. She succeeds in knocking you to the ground and jumps up on you again. This is when you struggle to look left and find the SAM switch. Bash the auto-aim button repeatedly until Bond mashes the button, which launches a rocket at the helicopter. The helicopter crash-lands and pulls Onatopp over the bridge with it, as she is still tethered to the crashing aircraft.

PAN AFRICA POWER SOLAR PARK

NORTHWEST NIGERIA

PRIMARY OBJECTIVES

Infiltrate the Pan-African Power Solar Plant

Destabilize the Solar Park Facility

Reach the Cradle Control Center

SECONDARY OBJECTIVE

Disable the Perimeter Defenses

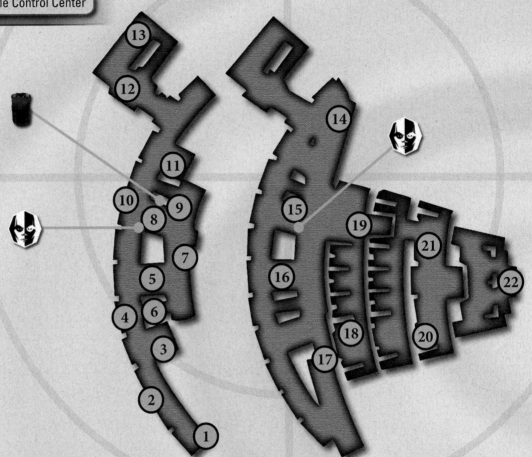

INFILTRATE THE PAN-AFRICAN POWER SOLAR PLANT

PAN-AFRICAN POWER SOLAR PLANT

Having traversed the Cuban Jungle and defeated Onatopp, Bond reaches the Pan Africa Power Solar Park facility. Avoiding the heavily guarded main gates, he discovers a maintenance hatch which he can use to stealthily gain entry to the complex. Once inside, Bond must infiltrate the Solar Park to confront Trevelyan and rescue Natalya.

You begin at the end of a dark hallway (**1**) with your smartphone and silenced P99. Two guards (**2**) work on consoles ahead. They are unaware of you. Crouch walk up close to them and shoot them both in quick succession to remain covert. Pick up their dropped **Masterton M-557** and **Hawksman M5A + Laser Pointer**.

Before you enter the next room (**3**) on the right, shoot the green-lit security cam in the back left corner. Silently shoot the patrolling soldier in the same hallway. Crouch walk into the room and silently subdue the guard while his attention is on the console.

Crouch walk out of the room (**4**) and turn right into the hallway (**6**) . Silently shoot or subdue the guard with his back to you here. Pivot right and shoot the patrolling soldier in front of the next room (**5**).

Use the hallway (**6**) to get behind the drone gun in the back hallway. Take out your smartphone and inch closer to the laptop (**7**). Hug the right wall so the drone gun does not track you. Convert the gun to your side by hacking the computer. This clears the hallway of enemies and even keeps you in stealth mode.

There's no need to go into the second room (**5**). If you do go in there from the back hallway make sure you shoot the security camera to the extreme right corner as you ease into the room.

Walk along the raised walkway on the left side of the hallway and peek into the room (8) at the bottom of the stairs. Shoot the soldier in the back right corner looking at a computer under a security camera. Shoot the man, then the camera.

Activate the drone gun looking through the "V" opening in the column near the doorway to the room. This clears the next hallway of enemies. Move into the room (8) to find a Janus symbol. You also find an **Armor** in the corner near the empty shelves.

JANUS SYMBOL #43
In the third room in the hallway you can find the Janus symbol inside the only open locker.

To get beyond the two drone guns at the end of the main hallway you must drop down into the maintenance hatch (10) in the middle of the hallway. Taking the **Kallos-TT9 with Silencer** lying in the hole is optional. Follow the short tunnel to a ledge; climb up and out of the tunnel to enter the next room (11).

Press the "Override" switch on the console below the hallway window. Watch as a piece of machinery pokes through a water chamber glass panel. The rush of water in the room knocks over and destroys the two troublesome drone guns.

Head to the next hallway corner and find cover to take down an entire squadron of soldiers in the next hallway (12). They take up positions on the high catwalk as well as on the lower floor. Some are exposed while some take cover.

Collect their weapons and expect two more soldiers to come running down the next hallway: one on the catwalk and later, one on the first floor. Follow the catwalk (13) to get off this floor. Shoot the security camera in the corner and then rush and shoot the next two guards in the last turn of the hallway. Shoot the padlock from the door at the end of the corridor to reach the solar panel array.

ACQUIRE EXPLOSIVE CHARGES
SOLAR PANEL ARRAY

Bond (14) receives an intelligence phone call from MI6. He is given the go ahead to destabilize the facility by detonating explosives within the Cooling Towers. Bond must move beyond the Solar Panel Array and take a maintenance lift down deeper in to the complex in order to rig it to explode.

AVOID RAISING AN ALARM
Being stealthy along the exterior of the Solar Panel Array is much easier than going in with guns blazing. You face more than double the amount of enemies if you go in with a bang.

Use a silencer on the guy at the top of the stairs (15). There are three more soldiers to deal with nearby. If you can take them all out without alerting their comrades, then the rest is cake.

Shoot the lone patrolling soldier and then reload and shoot the two soldiers standing next to each other in front of the weapons cache.

Do this without an alert and you can now grab the **sniper rifle** leaning up against the rail just before the small "bridge" in front of the weapons cache. Use the sniper rifle to take out all the remaining soldiers on the tiers below. Do this and you won't be bothered for a while. Do not ditch the sniper rifle if you want to remain unseen in this area. Consider trading your third weapon for one of the fine weapons in the weapons cache (16) up the steps.

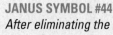

JANUS SYMBOL #44
After eliminating the soldiers in the area, turn back and look near the stairs you came up from. The Janus symbol is on the side of a stair rail column.

Continue to the next set of stairs (**17**) to reach the tier below. Activating the switch (**18**) at the first solar panel retracts the entire array on this level, which is interesting to watch. If you had not sniped everyone, there would be some resistance here and soldiers would cover between the solar panels or track columns.

When you reach the stairs (**19**) you can spot a couple of soldiers walking toward you from the next set of stairs (**20**) on the opposite side of the array. This happens even if you had previously sniped everyone.

To remain stealthy, use the silenced sniper rifle to drop one of the soldiers after another. Aim and shoot at the second target before the first one hits the ground to avoid detection. You can also move the solar array on this tier using the switch near the stairs (**19**).

Regardless of whether you remained stealthy or not, a single soldier walks out of a room under the previous tier as you approach the next set of stairs **(20)**. Shoot him quickly before he sees you.

A similar scenario plays out on the next level (no solar panels though). Snipe the two soldiers near the opposite staircase. Collect the three, time-triggered explosive charges **(21)** from the crate near the stairs.

The moment you take the charges, four enemy soldiers exit the elevator **(22)** on the lowest tier.

SABOTAGE THE COOLING TOWERS

Gun down the four soldiers from the elevator and then enter the elevator **(22)**. If you had not reached the explosives stealthily, there would have been a much bigger fight at this elevator. Activate the switch in the lift to head down to the cooling towers.

COOLING TOWERS

Guards patrol the cooling towers and are not aware of Bond until you break stealth. You must take out or bypass the guards and progress either left or right through the symmetrical upper gantries of the area to reach a service lift at the far end of the room.

You can take multiple routes to reach the lift, using the floors, gantry and platforms atop the cooling towers themselves as a means to traverse the environment. Enemies will patrol the area looking for you, and once spotted the area will become alerted and a gunfight ensues.

To remain stealthy, crouch-walk up to the guard with his back to you as you exit the lift. Subdue him and then take the sniper rifle leaning up against the rail. Silently snipe all the guards in the cooling tower through the lookout windows. Make sure to destroy the security cameras in the hallway that you choose to leave the area through.

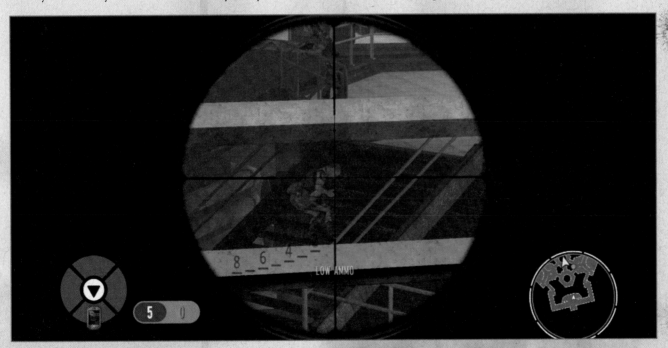

SECONDARY MISSION OBJECTIVE: DISABLE THE PERIMETER DEFENSES

Within the security control rooms to the east and west of the area, Bond can hack nodes located up above the observatory windows. Hack them to divert power away from the facility's perimeter defenses, allowing friendly units to breach the Solar Park facility. Shoot the security cameras inside the security rooms before entering. Performing two console hacks fully disables the perimeter fence and completes the level's secondary objective.

You must take the service elevator **(24)** down to reach the ground level of the facility in order to plant the explosives you just found. Activating the elevator alerts guards in the area, setting off sirens and flashing red lights. When this occurs, you must defend yourself while waiting for the lift to arrive. Dart to a security room for protection if you have trouble defending while standing at the lift.

JANUS SYMBOL #45

On the exit elevator side of the cooling chamber, stand on one of the adjacent balconies and look down at the pipes behind the elevator shaft. You can find this Janus symbol on the rooftop of the lower cooling tower entryway.

The elevator exits to a gantry, which leads in to a service room with two staircases to the ground level. Shoot the guard in the gantry as your elevator lowers to the first floor.

Enter the service room **(25)** and enemies storm in from the floors below. Three enemies appear on both sides of the room. A single enemy stands on the upper balcony on each side of the service room. Aim for those guys first, then target the two on the floor.

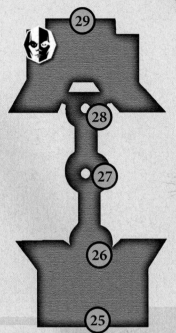

Enter the red-lit chamber in the middle of the service room. In the first tower chamber **(26)** you can find a place to set one of the explosives. Plant the explosive on the keypad on the right side of the tower core.

Continue forward and shoot the two soldiers that enter at the other end. Plant another charge on the second **(27)** and third **(28)** cores.

ENTER THE CRADLE

After exiting the cooling towers, guards attempt to stop you and try to safeguard the lift (29) to the surface. Two guards appear on the right side of the room and three on the left. Once you take out a couple of these goons, two more arrive via the exit lift.

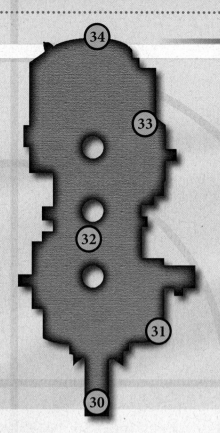

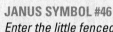

JANUS SYMBOL #46
Enter the little fenced office in the left corner, left of the exit lift. The Janus symbol is in a corner near the floor, between two storage bin shelves.

Enter the lift (29) and head to the Venting Area by activating the lift switch. Upon entering the lift, Bond sets a 20 second delay on the installed explosive charges.

VENTING AREA

Once the explosives are set, you must fight your way through the Venting Area to the Cradle in order to end Trevelyan's plan once and for all. To do this, you must first get through the largest number of enemies you've faced thus far. They fill the Venting Area as you take a few steps down the stairs (30).

Your first target should be the rocket-launching soldier on the corner of a rooftop on the right, then start prioritizing by the distance between you and the enemies filling the area. The rockets are your worst enemy right now. A good tactic is to run and gun as you aim straight ahead for the platform the two forward soldiers are standing on. If you get right under them, you can position a killing shot up at them before they can get a bead on you.

Another strategy is to take out the rocket-launching soldier and a few others on the right by exploding the truck (aim at the red gas tank) and then run right for the shelter **(31)** in the corner. There's a **Kallos-TT9** with grenade launcher in there in case you need more firepower. Grenades are good for large groups of enemies. Grenades are also a problem for you in this challenge. Make sure to keep your eye out for the grenade signal. Running away is the only option in that situation.

After clearing the entry area, more soldiers come out of the woodwork as you push forward toward the objective marker. You are forced to cross the middle platform **(32)** and zigzag through the area to get around obstructions. Expect heavy resistance from multiple levels as you move forward. Always use cover and only leave it when you pop up to get an auto target shot until the numbers of soldiers decrease and you can get a little more creative.

When you make it close to the end of the area **(33)** you initiate a very large battle with the last of the soldiers. Identify the worst threats and take them out in that order. Use explosive objects such as the transport truck to take out multiple enemies within proximity.

Run up the stairs and approach the elevator **(34)**. The level ends when you reach the Cradle's elevator entrance. Bond "accidentally" gets himself captured as three soldiers step off the lift and Bond does not attempt to resist. Bond starts the bomb timer as he hands over his smartphone to the soldiers.

PRIMARY OBJECTIVES

Defend Natalya

Get to the Machine Room

Deal with Trevelyan

Create a System Overload

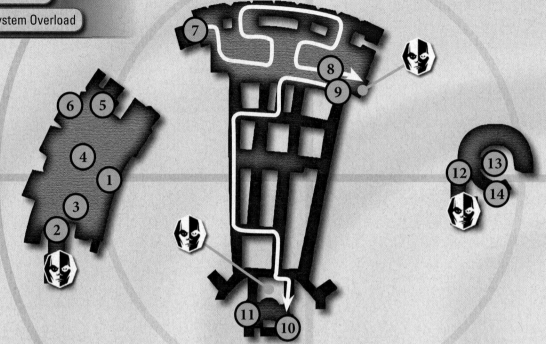

DEFEND NATALYA

GOLDENEYE CONTROL CENTER

Having made their way through the Solar Park, Bond and Natalya are taken as prisoners, Trevelyan reveals the hidden nature of the facility and his plans to use it to control the second GoldenEye Satellite and attack London.

As Trevelyan prepares to execute his diabolical scheme, he inadvertently creates enough of a diversion which allows Bond and Natalya to escape within the Control Room. Locked into the Control Room, Natalya attempts to stop the GoldenEye satellite while you defend her from Trevelyan's men who attempt to assault you and keep the computers from being hacked.

It all begins with your explosive charges going off, sending soldiers tumbling. Bond kicks the guard that led him into the center and steals his assault rifle. You **(1)** must gun down three soldiers pointing their guns at you in a slow-motion challenge. After taking them out, reload your weapon and pick up the dropped weapons. Sprint to catch up with Natalya.

Natalya is going to hack three computers in the room to stop the GoldenEye while waves of soldiers enter the room from random locations to try to stop her from succeeding. These soldiers target both you and the computer system she is working on. At the first computer **(2)**, try using the high catwalk platform as a great place to take out all the various waves of enemies. You can shoot just about any enemy spawn location from this high perch **(3)**.

Natalya cannot work on the computer if she is under attack. The hack meter at the top of the screen does not fill until she gets working. There's not only the survival component to deal with here; you have to have all three computers hacked before the light from the GoldenEye consumes the final computer, Natalya or you.

The key is to move quickly to defeat the guards so Natalya can move onto the next computer once the hacking meter at the top of the screen fills. Don't think you are buying time by allowing one distant soldier to live as he slowly makes his way to you. Hunt down the remaining soldiers in a wave and take them out to get the show on the road.

As she moves from computer to computer, pick up more weapons along the way. The same perch (3) used during the first computer hack position also works well for the second position (4) except when soldiers enter the room through the doors behind her. Shoot the soldiers that zipline through the windows first unless there is a soldier closer to the computer being hacked. Nailing the soldiers as they come through the window is much safer than once they are through and shooting back.

At the third computer location (5) it's good to stand near Natalya and watch for the soldiers that enter the room through the doors behind her and beside her. She has one last stop before the task is complete.

Natalya moves from the third computer to the small one (6) on the nearby wall. At this point you are safe from being annihilated by the light. But, despite Natalya's best efforts she discovers that Trevelyan still has control of the GoldenEye. Bond has no other choice but to fight his way out of the Control Rooms and stop Trevelyan on the exterior Corona Platform.

GET TO THE MACHINE ROOM

You now have four minutes to make it to the machine room. To reach this goal and find Janus symbols along the way, you're going to have to hurry. Don't spend time going out of your way for weapons in this control center. Head through the doorway behind the first computer (2). A Janus symbol is located in this small hallway.

JANUS SYMBOL #47

As you pass out of the control center through the sliding door near the first computer hack location (2), look back under the console on the left wall to find the Janus symbol.

CONTROL CENTER LOWER LEVEL

Bash the indicated shoulder buttons to pry open the elevator doors. Drop down into the shaft and then through the elevator access hatch below. This drops you into a room (7) where you can find two padlocked weapon chests. One chest contains two **Stauger UA-1s + Reflex Sights** while the other contains two **Terralite IIIs**.

There are no Janus symbols to be had in the burning lower level of the control center. Shoot the soldiers that get in your way as you sprint up the right catwalk, climb the stairs to the higher catwalk level and follow that to the exit stairs on the opposite side of the room. Continue shooting enemies as you avoid the fire and electrical hazards to follow the right platform to the exit **(8)**.

In the next small passageway you find a locked weapon chest containing two **Terralite III's**. There's also a Janus symbol in this small area that you can see much better just as you leave the room and look back.

JANUS SYMBOL #48

As you leave the small storage room near the burning lower control center level. Look under the leaning debris near the exit doorway. Shoot the symbol and keep going! The clock is still ticking.

GANTRIES

Bond (**9**) must fight Trevelyan's men as he makes his way to the Corona Platform's Machine Room (**10**). While traversing this location, sections of walkway fall away under Bond's weight. Trevelyan is also trying to hit Bond with a concentrated beam of sunlight from the collector at the top of the tower. If you are caught in one of the sections that collapses every time, press the indicated button to climb back up out of the hazard.

Follow the route we've marked on our map to get through the catwalk maze without incident. Make sure to pause from time to time to shoot nearby enemies or those that stand in your way. Sprint to the Machine Room (**10**) to complete the time-limit portion of this mission.

MACHINE ROOM

Trevelyan gets the drop on Bond in the Machine Room (**10**) and a hand-to-hand combat sequence ensues. The battle goes from a fistfight to a battle with a fire extinguisher, then to a fire axe. The button press sequence is a random order of three different buttons. Pay close attention to the onscreen prompts to make it through.

The battle ends with you being knocked down to a lower level of the Machine Room as you are thrown down into a pit. Climb the ladder out of the pit and exit the Machine Room.

JANUS SYMBOL #49

This Janus symbol rests between air ducts in a pit just outside of the Machine Room where you battle Trevelyan. It's best to get this symbol once the clock has stopped after the fight.

Follow the objective marker out of the Machine Room and back onto the gantries where you find a ladder (11) to a lower level. Vault over a low fence in this narrow chasm to drop down to the next level below where you can find the last Janus symbol.

214

JANUS SYMBOL #50

The final Janus symbol is located behind a fence next to some pipes in the Machine Room chasm. When you vault over your first fence on your way down to the lower level, look to the left and find this symbol near the corner. Shoot it through the chain-link.

Vault down another short fence and continue dropping down to the armory floor (12). You can find two weapon chests and a weapons locker in this room. Select an **SMG** and an **assault rifle** and make sure both are reloaded and full of ammo before leaving this room. Enter the observation room (13) where you must battle Trevelyan again.

DEAL WITH TREVELYAN

OBSERVATION ROOM: TREVELYAN FIGHT

Bond must defeat Trevelyan and his men while waiting for the lift to the bottom of the Corona (13). The fight within this room has three stages:

- Fighting Trevelyan alone
- Battling Trevelyan and some of his men
- Dealing with Trevelyan, some of his men, and an attack helicopter.

Much like the battle in the control center where you protected Natalya while she hacked computers, this battle pits you against waves of Trevelyan's soldiers. To get through this battle quickly, shoot Trevelyan when you can but focus on defeating each and every one of his soldiers in the different stages of the battle. Defeating his soldiers is key to reaching each next stage. If the next stage does not begin, you haven't subjected Trevelyan to enough damage.

It's convenient to use the exterior first and second level balconies for an escape from the many guns trained on you at one time, but you should avoid the balconies at all costs during the third stage with the attack helicopter. At this point you should be on the inside, first floor and behind the stack of crates that offers protection from soldiers' and the attack helicopter's attacks. Shoot Trevelyan after you've eliminated all the soldiers in the helicopter stage to trigger the next objective marker, the doorway **(14)** on the second level.

CREATE A SYSTEM OVERLOAD

ANTENNA CRADLE

After entering the objective marker lift **(14)**, press the indicated button to take the lift up to the Antenna Cradle. Bond needs to create a feedback loop at the Antenna Cradle to destroy the facility. Walk up to the keyboard on the opposite side of the central column. After pressing the indicated button to detonate, Trevelyan attacks you again, for the last time.

The fight with Trevelyan on the Antenna Cradle is similar to the previous fistfights, and, as before, the button press combination is random. Watch the bottom of the screen intently for the next command and try not to get caught up into the fight so much that you ignore a prompt for too long.

The final sequence of the fight is a battle over a dropped gun. When you press the correct button response Bond wins the battle.

MI6 OPS TIPS

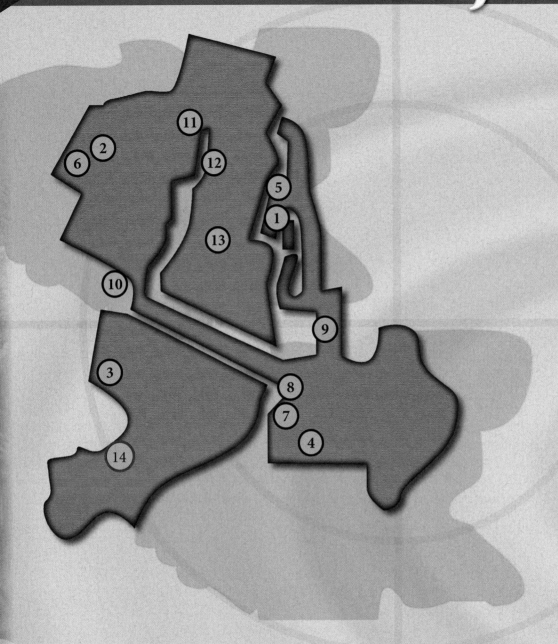

218

GAME TYPE   ELIMINATION

1. Base #1
2. NME Team Spawn (MP)
3. Base #2
4. MI6 Spawn Location
5. Base #1 Lower
6. NME Team Spawn (Lower) (MP)
7. MI6 Team Spawn (Lower) (MP)
8. MI6 Tunnel #1
9. MI6 Tunnel #2
10. NME Tunnel #1
11. NME Tunnel #2
12. Bridge
13. Truck
14. Front Gate

JUNGLE ELIMINATION TIPS

✳ Collect the shotgun and the assault rifle from the table in the beginning **(4)**.

✳ Rush out to the bridge **(12)** and shoot the truck **(13)** full of soldiers. Aim for the fuel tank.

✳ Shoot soldiers newly arriving from the front gate **(14)** from the vantage point of the bridge.

✳ Use the tunnels **(8 – 11)** to recover from wounds.

✳ Use the explosive barrels to your advantage.

✳ Keep your weapons fresh. Find weapon crates in all the buildings and in the tunnels near the control rooms.

✳ Make snipers your priority targets. Snipers are usually on the highest level and on high ledges and rooftops that you can't even get to. Use the tunnels to sneak up on them.

✳ The enemy rarely sees you through an unbroken window.

✳ When you are down to the last handful of targets, head up to high ground. Use rooftops or the bridge to draw them out. This also gives you the height advantage once you've spotted them.

MEMORIAL

MAP HIGHLIGHTS

1. Entrance (MI6 Ops)
2. Right Console, Drone Gun & Drone Gun Laptop
3. Left Console, Drone Gun & Drone Gun Laptop
4. Ruins Platform Console, Drone Gun & Laptop

GAME TYPE — DEFENSE

In this Defense style map, you must protect three consoles from enemy attacks while you download the data. You can approach the three data consoles in any order. When you start a download, hostiles are deployed and you must try to destroy them.

The data transfer takes 3 minutes. During this time you must protect the console from enemy attacks. Watch the console health bar at the top of the screen. If it falls to zero before the data is transferred the mission fails.

- Use the three drone guns to your advantage. Smartphone hack the nearby laptop to turn it on.
- Drone gun operation time is limited (good for one and a half rounds) so use them when you need them the most. There is one well-positioned drone gun for each console location.
- Make sure you have a good loadout before you start the data transfer. Keep this in mind as you complete one transfer and start the next.
- Save the data console on the ruins temple platform (4) for last; it's the easiest to defend. You simply move between guarding the interior stairwell and shooting from the console's ledge.

- If you stay near the console then you know where the priority enemies are lurking. The drawback is that you are also an easy target.
- If you keep the data console close in sight but stand at a distance behind enemy lines, you can drop a lot of unsuspecting enemies. The drawback is that reinforcements may come up behind you on their way to the front line.
- Pump the trigger on assault rifles to increase accuracy and to conserve precious ammo.

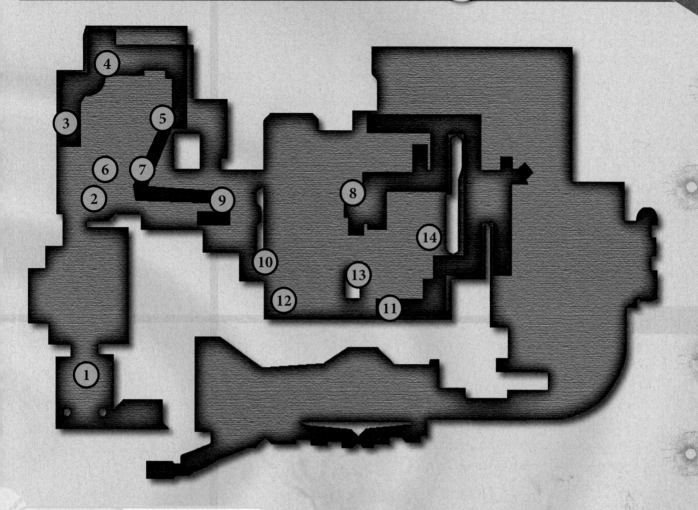

GAME TYPE — DEFENSE

MAP HIGHLIGHTS

1. MI6 Ops Start Location
2. Walkthrough Tip
3. Ops Escalator
4. Second Story Sniper
5. Walkthrough Tip
6. Walkthrough Tip
7. Scaffold Bridge
8. Second Story Sniper
9. Scaffold Corner w/Ladder
10. Scaffold Corner
11. Distant Sniper
12. Snipe Position
13. Weapon Chest Tunnel
14. Forklift Tip

This is a stealth mission with a set number of enemies no matter what enemy amount you choose in the options. We also suggest not attempting to complete this in the early stages of your discovery of this mission with the Ragdoll option on. When enemies go flying when you kill them, it's hard to remain stealthy.

✳ Be careful with the sniper rifle that you don't shoot so far out into a distant area that you can't tell if the target has a witness.

✳ Having Radar Dots Always On is a good idea when you are first learning the turf.

In the first room (**1**) creep walk up to the guard leaning on a half-wall and subdue him. Subdue the next closest guy near the drone gun laser light. Use your smartphone to hack the laptop. The gun goes down temporarily. Creep walk past its usual scan zone and subdue the next two guards with their backs to you near the large exit (**2**).

If you did that like clockwork from the start, the last guard in the area is still walking up the escalator (**3**). Shoot him silently before he rounds the corner on the second floor. If he gets to the end of his route he stands next to a sniper (**4**).

If this happens, it's okay. You can come up behind them while crouch walking through the open floor behind them. Sneak up behind both and subdue the guard and then the sniper. Otherwise, shoot the guy on the escalator and then shoot the sniper in the head.

Look for the guard in the distance walking along a second story catwalk bridge. Shoot him when he stops on your side of the bridge. Take the dropped sniper rifle, the **AS15 MK12 + Silencer**.

There are two patrolling guards in the construction area below. Stand where the sniper was standing (4) and first shoot the guard coming through a garage below (5) to your extreme left. Shoot the other patrolling guard as he walks behind the pallet full of concrete slabs (6). This keeps his death out of the view of the next guard on a platform looking in his direction.

Follow the upper level to the catwalk bridge where you shot the patrolling guard. Crouch up to the corner where you shot him and look down. First shoot the farther guard facing your direction (he's not looking up) and then the second guard on the lower platform (7).

Stay in the same position (7) and look through the scope. Find the sniper in the distance (8) on the far back scaffold structure, across the next clearing.

Follow the catwalk to the next corner (9) where you can spot six soldiers guarding the pit area down below. To catch them unawares, you need to snipe them in a specific order. Keep in mind that if one guard sees the other drop, then it's all over. So, shoot the guy with his back to you (a), which is also the closest to you. He's watching all the guards in the pit.

Next, shoot the guard (b) in the barricaded area closest to you and walking toward the group (d) of three guards. Two of these guards stay facing each other while the third continues off on his patrol route. If he (b) gets too close to the group, do not shoot. Save him for later—further in his patrol route. Next shoot the distant guard (c) to the far left in the construction yard. Shoot him when he is to the farthest left point in his patrol route.

Use the ladder to get off the scaffold in your corner (9). Follow the hallway to the right under the scaffold to progress. If you did not kill soldier (b) previously, then find him at the end of his patrol route through a crack in the corner (10) of the building and the edge of the next scaffold catwalk. Make sure you are close enough to the crack to shoot above collision detection areas.

Look up and across the construction yard to a distant guard (11) on the right who is facing left. Make sure that there is not a patrolling guard near him when you shoot him.

Remain at the corner. Look over the left rail of the scaffold and finish off the two guards (d) facing each other that you missed earlier. To do this successfully, make sure you reload the sniper rifle, take aim and shoot one guard and immediately shoot the next before the alarm is set off.

Use the same technique to take out the two guards facing each other. Do this from the next scaffold corner (12). The two guards are sometimes hard to spot. They wear dark clothing and stand in the shadow of a pile of girders.

Follow the scaffold around the corner and vault over to reach the ground below. Double back to the left to find a tunnel that leads to a weapon chest (13) with another sniper rifle, the **AS15 MK 12 + Multiple Attachments**.

From the entrance to the weapon chest tunnel you can see an opening in a wall section to another section of the site, marked by a forklift (14) and a patrolling guard. Snipe the guard near the forklift. Also notice the few soldiers on top of the distant scaffold.

Get behind the forklift (14) and notice the remaining four guards in the area. One is on the ground under the scaffold platform beyond the drone gun, the rest are on top. Snipe the guard on the ground first.

From the corner of the forklift (14), snipe the three guards patrolling the top of the scaffold platform above the drone gun. Watch their patterns and shoot them when they are walking away from another guard. Don't let any one guard see the other drop. Shoot or hack the laptop on the cable spool to shut down the drone gun, also on the cable spool.

Pass under the scaffold and don't go up the ramp. Instead, follow the tunnel slope under the scaffold platform. The last two enemies stand next to each other facing away from you inside the tunnel. Snipe them both in quick succession to complete the level.

NIGHTCLUB

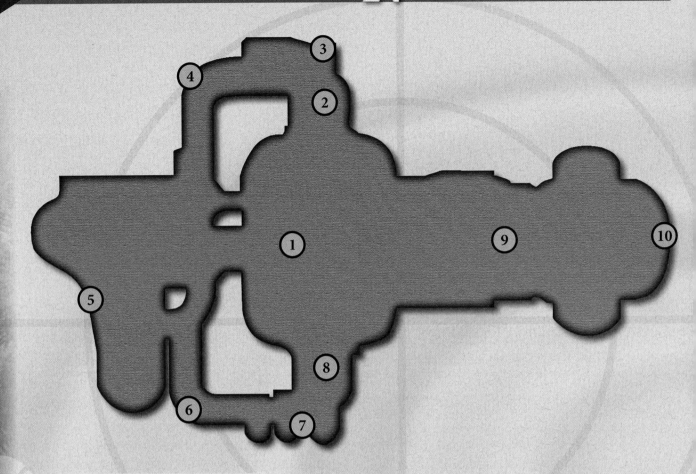

| GAME TYPE | ELIMINATION |

MAP HIGHLIGHTS

1 Dance Floor

2 Upper Balcony North

3 Chill Out Area North

4 Neon Corridor North

5 Green Room

6 Neon Corridor South

7 Chill Out Area South

8 Upper Balcony South

9 Office

10 Pink Room

This visit to the nightclub is an elimination event. As soon as you leave the spawn area (9) hostiles deploy into the level. You must take them out as quickly as you can to get the highest score possible. Find the **Kallos-TT9** on the pink sofa near the staging area. There's also a **Torka T3** and a **Sly 2020** shotgun on the same couch.

⊕ You can vault over second floor rails to reach the lower dance floor **(1)**.

⊕ There is a rail gun in the middle of the dance floor **(1)** in the DJ booth. Use the smartphone to hack the laptop to have the gun work for you temporarily.

⊕ Keep moving frequently between floor levels to keep the enemy disorganized while trying to clear a section at a time.

⊕ From the highest level above the dance floor **(1)** you can climb up on and travel along the round light and speaker truss.

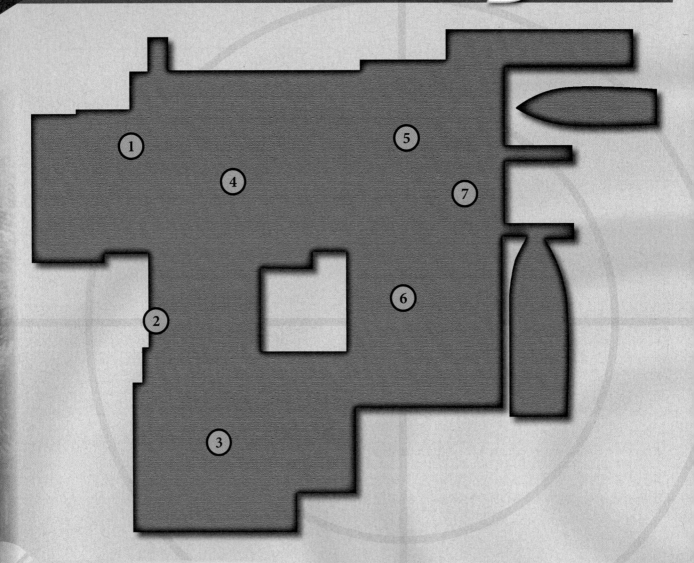

GAME TYPE | DEFENSE

MAP HIGHLIGHTS

1. Garage
2. Ambush Room
3. Boatyard
4. Courtyard

5. Dockside Interior #1
6. Dockside Interior #2
7. Dockside

COURTYARD

You can find a nice selection of weapons in an open weapon locker at the start position (**a**). Defending the console (**b**) on a porch in the left courtyard is pretty fun. On one end of the console porch is a **Vargen FH-7 with scope** in a weapon case and at the other end of the porch is a ladder. Climb the ladder at the end of the porch to use the balcony above as a defensive base. The railings do a pretty good job of stopping bullets. Strafe continually, crouching at times to avoid attacks, and make yourself a tougher target.

BOATYARD

Successfully defend the Boatyard console (**d**) by holding your ground in the vicinity of the console, using the line of various objects in the middle of the yard as cover. The enemy enters the area through one of three entry points. The first can be found on the ground to your right when you're facing the apartment building from the console, through the gate opening. The other two entry points are through windows of the second floor apartment building.

When you see enemies pile out of windows, drop everything to make that your primary target as you can take out many enemies quickly by targeting one location. Try to keep all enemies out of your gated area and you do fine. Move from one side of the central mound of objects to defend both gate entrances. Also try to take out the four enemies inside the helicopter before they rappel to the ground.

DOCKS

The docks console is the easiest to defend. The enemy enters the office area through the "Sortie" doorway facing the water or through one of two doors on the left. One door is marked "Entrepot" and third door is in the corner to the left of this door. If you stand your ground beside the console so that you can quickly cover any of these entrances, then you've got it made. If you get overpowered, back up out of the narrow door behind the console and come back and retake the area when you are ready.

GAME TYPE **STEALTH**

MAP HIGHLIGHTS

 Walkthrough Tips

DISPATCH ALL ENEMIES COVERTLY

You begin this stealth mission inside a small storage room (1) in the machine shops on the Airfield map. You must dispatch all the enemies in the level without being spotted (or setting off alarms).

Open the door and crouch walk behind the crates in the next room (2). Shoot the first soldier you see. He's the one to the left of others while looking at the radar.

Strafe to the gap between the double stack of crates and the single crate. Shoot the nearby soldier with his back to you in the back of the head with a silenced shot, as well. Keep an eye on the patrolling guard. He starts on this floor, walks up the stairs and stands on the second level in the next room (also with his back to you). He can spot you from the catwalk so don't move or shoot anyone when he is facing you.

Strafe out into the room and spot three guards in the next room (3) through an open doorway. If you stand up you can see the guard that moved upstairs. Silently shoot him in the head.

Move to the second doorway (the leftmost door) that leads from the garage into the next room (3). From the doorway, silently headshot the guard near the forklift.

Crouch-walk up to the forklift. Face the patrolling guard in the room when he stops near the doorway to the garage. Pop him in the head when he stops walking.

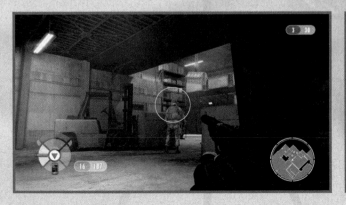

Now that the room is clear except for the two guards standing next to each other, aim and shoot at the red winch holding the engine block above these two soldiers' heads. The engine block crushes both of them—not too silent, but it gets the job done without alarms.

That clears this area. Now you need to head outside where you have a choice of routes. We suggest you remain on the first floor. Head into the small storage room (4) using the door behind the forklift.

Open the next door to reach the exterior and remain crouched and in the doorway. Look left and you see three soldiers (5) with their backs to you. Shoot the leftmost guard at the bottom of the stairs first. Allow the middle guard to get to his destination beside the parked Humvee and then shoot the rightmost guard, near the broken column, in the head.

Crouch walk up the stairs to your left that lead up to the upper machine shop doorway. There's a sniper up high on a ledge that you can see from the top of the stairwell. Shoot him in the head with the silenced P99.

Walk up to the railing on the stairwell that is closest to the sniper you just shot and stand up. Look down over the railing and you spot a drone gun laptop and a soldier (6) staring at it. Shoot this guy in the head with a silenced round. The railing is high, so to shoot over it, look down your sights for this shot. Do not hack the drone gun laptop yet; there are too many soldiers for it to shoot. Doing so now sets off an alarm.

Head back down the stairs and crouch walk up to the parked Humvee while looking for that one guard of the first three exterior guards you saw when you exited the shop. He's standing on the blind side of the Humvee with his back to you. Come up behind him and subdue him or shoot him in the head with a silenced round.

Crouch walk to the open doorway of the drone enclosure (7) and shoot the standing soldier inside. Do not enter this room. Instead, head back up the stairwell and look at the drone gun laptop with your smartphone. You can hack the laptop from here. Activating the drone gun now eliminates the two remaining soldiers near the rollup door (8).

Another soldier exits the building through the door on the left as you approach the rollup door. He's alone, so it's an easy kill.

Enter the doorway he came through **(9)**. Head through the connecting rooms until you arrive at the slightly opened rollup door **(10)** in front of the parked transport truck. From here you can silently shoot a soldier to your extreme right as well as the nearby soldier on your left behind the barricade which you need to move to next **(11)**.

From behind the barricade **(11)**, find the outline of a soldier at the second level railing above the bunker near the SAM launcher. Take careful aim and put a silenced bullet in his head.

Quickly approach the entrance to the bunker **(12)** but stop short of entering while upright. Crouch down at the entrance and either shoot the guard at the lookout window or subdue him.

Slowly climb the stairs in the bunker **(12)** and stop as your head crests the rooftop so you can see over the SAMs and to the adjacent balcony **(13)**. Shoot the soldier's head you can see poking above the short wall on the balcony.

Head up onto the SAM rooftop and back down the next set of stairs on the other side. Climb the adjacent stairwell to reach the platform where you killed the last soldier **(13)**. On this balcony you find two, silenced **ANOVA DP3s**. Take one, reload and take another. Remain on this balcony, behind the entryway columns, until a patrolling guard passes by. Get behind him while crouching, catch up to him, match his speed and then subdue him.

Through the doorways on the left, you hear the voices of more soldiers. Don't go through those doors **(16)** just yet. Continue down the stairs headed for the burning crash site. While looking over the rail at the large fires, spot the two soldiers kicking in the ashes with their backs to you. Shoot the guy on the left then the one on the right. There are two more soldiers just around the left corner inside the building **(14)** but you can see them through the large crash site hole in the wall. Shoot them both from the last step looking back through the crash site hole. Shoot the closest one first.

Head around the debris and enter the building through this hole **(14)**. Climb the stairs **(15)** and shoot the patrolling soldier in the back of the head. You notice two more guards ahead of that soldier. They stand guard shoulder to shoulder at that doorway **(16)** you passed earlier. Backtrack through the hole, up the staircase and to these double doors.

Open the doors **(16)** and shoot them both in quick succession. There's one more soldier on this level. He's around the left corner near the stairs. Shoot him quickly as you round the corner. He was the last man standing.

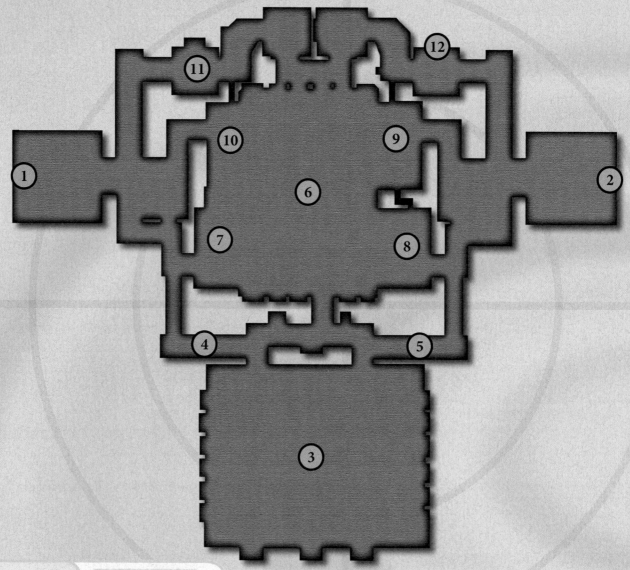

GAME TYPE — ELIMINATION

MAP HIGHLIGHTS

1. MI6 Team Spawn (MP)
2. NME Team Spawn (MP)
3. Large Room
4. Access Corridor 1
5. Access Corridor 2
6. Core room
7. Lab 1
8. Lab 2
9. Lab 3
10. Lab 4
11. Overlook left
12. Overlook right

FACILITY TIPS

When you begin this challenge you are reminded that there are drone guns in the area and that you can use your smartphone to hack the laptops to take control of those guns for yourself. The laptop locations are marked on our map. You start this mission in the same place you would in multiplayer, in the MI6 Spawn room **(1)**.

Before you leave the first room, grab the **Anova DP3** and the **SEGS 550**—hang on to that one. It's a slugger.

The first drone gun is in a room you reach by taking passages to the right as you exit the spawn room. You find the drone gun laptop (7) in the first lab room on the right by another set of stairs. Don't activate it until you've got a crowd to witness it.

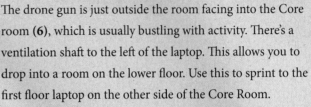

The drone gun is just outside the room facing into the Core room (6), which is usually bustling with activity. There's a ventilation shaft to the left of the laptop. This allows you to drop into a room on the lower floor. Use this to sprint to the first floor laptop on the other side of the Core Room.

Grenades and Remote Mines come in handy on this map. If you've found a good choke point to filter the enemies through you want to make sure you have an exit plan or just have your backside covered. Drop the remote mine down an adjacent hallway and watch the radar. When a crowd forms, detonate it by pressing down on the D-Pad. You are given three of these, as well as three Grenades.

On the highest point on the yellow metal platform in the middle of the Core Room (6) is a ladder near the stairwell. Climb this ladder to the top and you discover a network of catwalks and pipes that encompasses the entire area. You can get the drop on a lot of enemies using this vantage point.

In the last wave of attacks you must go up against the elite guards in hazmat gear. They're a little more armored and aggressive than the previous soldiers.

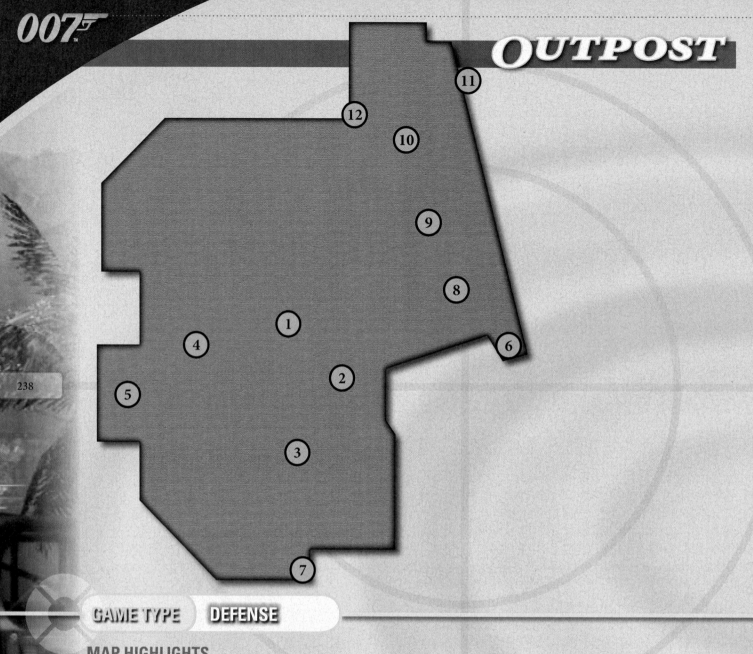

GAME TYPE DEFENSE

MAP HIGHLIGHTS

1. Central Hut
2. Hut 1
3. Radio Mast
4. MIG
5. Burned Building
6. Guard Tower 1
7. Guard Tower 2
8. Hut 2
9. Hut 3
10. Large Hut
11. Guard Tower 3
12. Satellite Dish Stairwell

BURNING BUILDING

You start this mission beside the first console (**a**) next to the burning building. Pick up the dropped weapons that litter the area and then activate the download on the console. The first thing you should do is target and kill the sniper in the guard tower (**7**).

The rest of the wave enters the area through the Radio building (3) and the adjacent open shipping container. Clear this wave and quickly get to the top of the guard tower (7). From here you can easily defend the console from the remaining waves. You can also use the **WA2000 + Thermal Scope** that the sniper dropped in there.

RADIO MAST

Defending the radio house's console (b) can be tricky. Using the same tower (7) is good for holding enemies at a distance from the house, but once one gets through you are stuck on the ground defending anyway since you can shoot inside the house from the tower.

The enemy populates from the structures on the right side of the map **(8), (9) & (10).** Make your stand at the doorway facing this location, shooting through the open shipping container. The shipping container is also good for protection once the enemies are in your zone. Use it to come up behind the enemy line.

The enemy crowds into the house and shoots the console point blank if you allow them. Stay close to the house but continue to move around and through the house to defend it properly. You can find a **Stauger UA-1 with Reflex Sight** in a weapon chest inside this structure (3).

SATELLITE FACILITY

On the rooftop of the Satellite Facility (10)(where the dish is located) you can find a weapon chest with an **Ivana Spec-R with multiple attachments**. Defend this structure's balcony console (c) by using the rooftop as your main defense base. From here you can take out all enemies around and those that gather close to the console by just peering over the edge of the roof. The only problem is the enemy often gets on the floor below you on the same level as the console. You have to move to clear out the areas directly below you from time to time. You can vault over the edge or use the stairs to move quickly between levels.

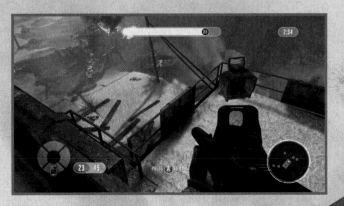

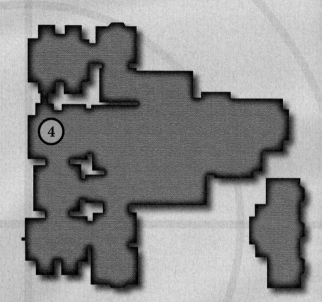

GAME TYPE | ELIMINATION

MAP HIGHLIGHTS

1 Blue Base (MI6 Multiplayer Spawn Room)

2 Stauger AU-1 Room with ventilation access to lower floor

3 Mobile light Room with ventilation to lower floor

4 Sigmus 9 weapon case room with escape hatch

You begin this challenge on the second floor in the MI6 Multiplayer base **(1)**. There's a weapon case with a **Stauger UA-1** and a **Hawksman M5A**. Leave the pistol and also take the **PT-9 Interdictus** from the gun rack on the other side of the room. Leave the room to begin the battle.

Besides the stairs, there are a few ventilation shafts that allow you quick access to the floor below. You can find one of these in the same room (2) with the Stauger AU-1 weapon case on the second floor. Look behind the stack of boxes.

You can find another vent shaft to the lower floor in the mobile light room (3). Look behind the oddly stacked tables in the corner.

In a lower floor room (4), you can find an escape route through a small vent-like opening in the corner adjacent to the **Sigmus 9** weapon case. In the last wave of attacks you must go up against the elite guards in riot gear. They're a little more armored and aggressive than the previous soldiers.

GAME TYPE **STEALTH**

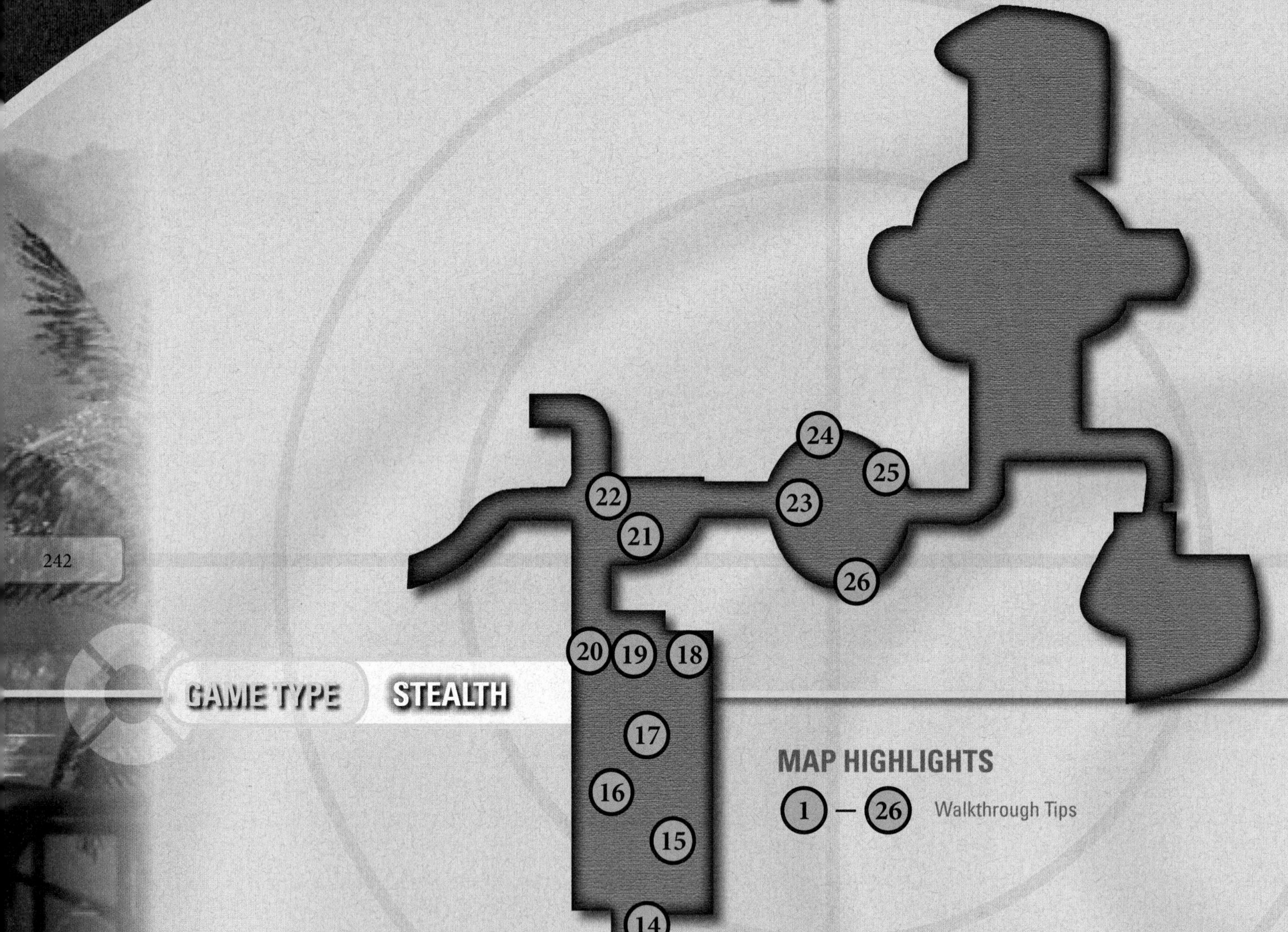

MAP HIGHLIGHTS

(1) — (26)   Walkthrough Tips

You begin this mission in the hallway (1) attached to the restaurant. Through the first doorway is the restaurant filled with enemies. Begin by pushing through the door and crouch walking to the enemy (2) with his back to you near a table. Next, follow the guard walking up the stairs to your left on his (3) patrol route.

Now subdue the man (4) leaning on the balcony railing looking down into the restaurant below. Use the door near this guard to enter the storage room with vent access. Follow the vent (5) to the security room. Silently shoot the man through the hole in the floor and then drop down into the room.

Exit the room through the door and use the vent to cut the blocked hallway. Follow the stairs to a room with two enemies and a security camera. Shoot the man (6) walking out of the room as you arrive. Shoot the man (7) near the security camera and then shoot the camera.

Exit the room and enter the door on the right. You are now reentering the restaurant on the second floor balcony (8). Subdue the man (9) looking over the rail near the stairs. Back away from the rail; there are still a few enemies below.

Move back toward the entrance (8) to this balcony. Approach the rail overlooking the restaurant from this location and silently shoot the guard below, leaning on a rail looking out into the seating area. Look directly down and to your left to find the security camera above the bar. Shoot it. Look down and to your extreme right and shoot the enemy (11) behind the bar facing the inside wall.

This leaves three men in the restaurant. They are grouped together in an area (12) below your balcony stairs. If you approach the stairs, one of the guards begins a patrol route and begins to head for your stairs. Back up to the previous hallway (6) through the unlocked door. Watch the man's patrol route. When he stops near the same door, open it up and shoot him quickly and silently.

Now you can walk further along the second floor balcony and pass the balcony stairs to find a position right above the two guards (12) remaining in the restaurant. Shoot them both in quick succession with the silenced P99.

Now leave the restaurant through the door **(13)** behind the bar. Shoot the security camera **(14)** in the corner above the door to the kitchen. Headshot the two guards in the kitchen, starting with the closest guard first. If the patrolling guard is nearby, wait until he has moved on. Shoot the security camera up around the first corner to the left**(15)**.

Shoot the patrolling guard in the back before leaving the kitchen entry position. Look around the first left corner in the kitchen and shoot the closest guard on the left, leaning up against a wall **(16)**.

Approach the second large stove in the middle of the room and shoot the guard **(17)** on the other side through the shelving on the large stove assembly. Next, shoot the security camera on the wall behind him.

Exit the kitchen through the back right corner doorway **(18)**. You catch two guards in a walk-in refrigerator with their backs to you. Shoot them both in quick succession.

Open the next door to exit the refrigerator when the patrolling guard in the next room is to the right inspecting some shelves. Open the door and shoot or subdue him **(19)**. You can now spot another guard looking out of an observation window in the corner of this room and yet another in the next hallway through this window.

Subdue the remaining guard in your room and then quickly shoot the man **(20)** in the hallway through the window before the alarm is triggered. Before you open the hallway door, shoot through the broken window to take out the security camera in the hallway corner.

Open the hallway door and shoot or subdue the man **(21)** to the right behind a small bar counter. Enter the room and hide behind the closest side of the same bar counter. Crouch walk around it to avoid the two patrolling guards entering the room. One guard stops and the other continues walking beyond a security camera. Shoot the closest man **(22),** then the other, then finally the security camera.

Now you're ready for the bathroom challenge. Shoot the first two guards **(23)** you see in quick succession. This leaves three men remaining. Two are inside stalls on opposite sides of the round bathroom. The farthest guard is the one not inside a stall. So, crouch walk left and allow the stall door to open and the guard to walk out. He **(24)** walks away from you. Shoot him quickly.

Head to the end of the round stall hallway wall and subdue the guard **(25)** leaning up against the end of the wall. Finally, head to the other side of the room to the other stalls and shoot the man **(26)** that exits the stall to complete the mission.

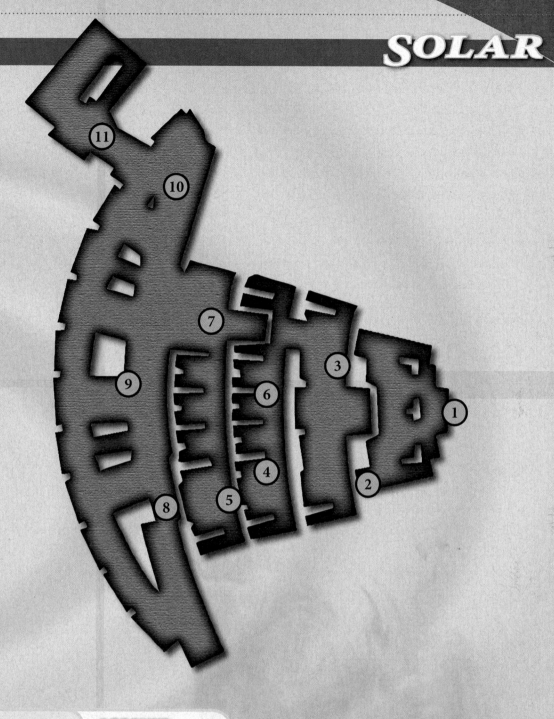

MI-6 OPS

GAME TYPE ASSAULT

MAP HIGHLIGHTS

1. MI6 OPS Start location

2. Weapon storage: Kallos-TT9 + Reflex Sight

3. Tier One

4. Second Tier

5. Weapon storage: Ivana Spec-R + ACOG Scope

6. Drone gun

7. Third Tier

8. Weapon storage: Ivana Spec-R + Reflex Sight and a Kallos-TT9 + Multiple

9. Weapon pit: MJR-409 (rocket launcher)

10. Stairwell hall (final helicopter battle)

11. Exit hallway

ELEVATOR BATTLE

You begin this challenge on the lift on the lowest level of the Solar Panel Array. When the elevator doors open, shoot the two guards standing at the lift in the slow-motion challenge. Take one of their **Kallos-TT9's** and quickly shoot the soldier on the stairs and the one near the forklift at the top of the right staircase. Exit the elevator just enough to shoot the men rappelling out of the helicopter before they deploy.

There are two soldiers on your level. Both are behind objects that keep them from moving in on you from the start. Hunt them down now and inspect the left storage room **(2)** under the first tier.

Each tier of the solar panel array is like a battle stage and most of these stages begin with a helicopter drop. If you have the rhythm of the challenge down pat then you can usually manage to eliminate all the soldiers in the helicopters before they drop, without too much ground resistance.

If you just missed that opportunity to shoot sitting ducks, then toss a grenade on the soldiers' landing zone. The ones on the ground are slow to scramble and the ones rappelling can do nothing to avoid the blast. Use the weapon shelter and the room on the opposite end for cover. Once you eliminate enough enemies to push up onto the next tier, do so.

TIER ONE BATTLE

When no more enemies spawn while battling on the elevator level of the array, move up the stairs to the first tier **(3)** and take out the one or two soldiers that usually do not venture down the stairs to hunt you down. Finishing off all the soldiers initiates the next stage of the battle…

Sniper Stage

As soon as you finish off the first wave of attacks, two snipers appear on the edge of the second tier with their laser sniper scopes searching for you. If you find cover using one of the large columns under them you are in good shape. You can often gun down both snipers before either one of them gets a bead on you.

Second Tier Attack Wave

The next attack is similar to the first: a helicopter drops soldiers on the far right end of the second tier while other ground troops fill the walkways above. If after defeating the snipers you worked your way to the right end (**3**) of the first tier then you are in a great position to take out the soldiers in the chopper.

There are weapons in racks near the storage shelter on this end (**3**). There are no guns in the shelter. You have a choice of the **Masterton M-557** and the **AS 15 mk 12** sniper rifle. You can hold down the entire wave from around this location. Watch the stairs at the left end of the tier and above your head from soldiers shooting over the rails.

A second wave starts with a helicopter drop around the middle of the third tier (**7**). This is an indication that it's time to move up to the second tier (**4**) using the stairs on the left end.

TIER TWO BATTLE

Run up the stairs (**4**) and make a beeline for the weapons storage (**5**) to collect an **Ivana Spec-R + ACOG Scope** from the weapons rack. The quickest way to clear this stage is to run around the large column at the weapon storage and work your way beyond the first solar panel track divider. Crouch down as soon as you can to avoid the drone gun's attack. The drone gun (**6**) is on the walkway around the middle of the tier.

Hop from divider to divider until you are one away from where the laptop sits. You can use your smartphone to hack the drone gun from one column away. Hack it and the drone gun turns on any enemies it sees on the second and third tier.

TIER THREE BATTLE

Continue to the stairs on the right end of the second tier to reach the third tier (**7**). This battle is similar to the previous one. Get to the solar panel columns to gain cover from another drone gun attack. The gun and the laptop are in similar positions as you found on the lower tier. Gun down the helicopter drop above the fourth tier while crouching behind a column.

Hack the laptop to force the drone gun to turn on its owners. While the drone gun is shooting, run up the stairs to the covered stairwell. There are two weapon cases at the stairs (**8**). They contain an **Ivana Spec-R + Reflex Sight** and a **Kallos-TT9 + Multiple**.

TIER FOUR: TOP OF THE SOLAR ARRAY

Helicopter Battle

Slowly climb the stairs and gun down the remaining soldiers from the top of the array. When all the soldiers are gone, dash for the rocket launcher weapon pit **(9)** beside the small walkway bridge. Duck down. An attack helicopter appears and unloads on you. The pit keeps you safe. Pick up the **MJR-409** from one of the two rocket launcher cases in the pit. If you run out of ammo during this fight, strafe back to the case and pick up another rocket launcher.

Stay crouched at the pit wall. When the helicopter fire seizes for a reload, pop up and shoot a rocket at the helicopter. Hit it three times and it flies off and leaves you alone for a moment. Keep the rocket launcher with you and reload an assault rifle for the next fight.

FOURTH TIER STAIRWELL

Head down the stairs with the rocket launcher equipped and ready. As you approach the forklift in the long stairwell hallway, soldiers begin filling the room **(10)** and ziplining through the windows on the right. Fire a rocket or two into the crowd and then switch over to the assault rifle to prepare for the second wave. Use the forklift as cover from both the forces and the helicopter that has reappeared outside.

After clearing the room of soldiers, find **Rocket Launcher ammo** in the weapon chests besides the stairs. Use these rockets to shoot down the helicopter once and for all. Hit it three times to finish it. Quickly follow the directional marker on the radar to the hallway exit **(11)** to complete the mission.

ACHIEVEMENTS & TROPHIES

	Name	Description	Xbox 360 Gamer Points	PS3 Trophy Type
	MI6 Ops Recruit	Earn 10 stars in MI6 Ops.	10	Bronze
	MI6 Ops Specialist	Earn 25 stars in MI6 Ops.	25	Silver
	MI6 Ops Elite	Earn 44 stars in MI6 Ops.	45	Gold

COMPLETING THE GAME

	Name	Description	Xbox 360 Gamer Points	PS3 Trophy Type
	Operative	Complete all objectives for every mission on Operative difficulty.	10	Bronze
	Agent	Complete all objectives for every mission on Agent difficulty.	15	Bronze
	007	Complete all objectives for every mission on 007 difficulty.	25	Silver
	Classic	Complete all objectives for every mission on 007 Classic difficulty.	40	Gold

COMPLETING MILESTONES

	Name	Description	Xbox 360 Gamer Points	PS3 Trophy Type
	Arkhangelsk Dossier	Complete all objectives in Arkhangelsk on 007 difficulty or higher.	40	Bronze
	Barcelona Dossier	Complete all objectives in Barcelona on 007 difficulty or higher.	15	Bronze
	Dubai Dossier	Complete all objectives in Dubai on 007 difficulty or higher.	15	Bronze
	Severnaya Dossier	Complete all objectives in Severnaya on 007 difficulty or higher.	30	Silver
	St. Petersburg Dossier	Complete all objectives in St. Petersburg on 007 difficulty or higher.	40	Silver
	Nigeria Dossier	Complete all objectives in Nigeria on 007 difficulty or higher.	40	Silver

KILLS IN SPECIFIC WAYS

	Name	Description	Xbox 360 Gamer Points	PS3 Trophy Type
	Phone a Friend	Get 20 kills with hacked sentry guns in 'Jungle.'	15	Bronze
	Bullet Dance	Get 40 kills with the Wolfe .44 in 'Nightclub.'	20	Bronze
	Rocket Man	Kill an enemy with the RPG in 'Dam.'	15	Bronze
	Royal Flush	In 'Facility,' successfully kill the enemy in the toilet cubicle without any shots being fired.	2	Bronze

HIDDEN TARGETS

	Name	Description	Xbox 360 Gamer Points	PS3 Trophy Type
	Emblem Hunter	Single Player: Find and destroy a Janus emblem.	5	Bronze
	Emblem Marksman	Single Player: Find and destroy 20 Janus emblems.	10	Bronze
	Emblem Elite	Single Player: Find and destroy 50 Janus emblems.	15	Silver

SKILLS

	Name	Description	Xbox 360 Gamer Points	PS3 Trophy Type
	I am INVINCIBLE!	Single Player: Complete any mission without taking any damage.	25	Bronze
	Dressed to Kill	Single Player: Complete any mission without collecting any body armor on 007 Classic difficulty.	20	Bronze

STEALTH

	Name	Description	Xbox 360 Gamer Points	PS3 Trophy Type
	Going Dark	Get to master engineering in 'Facility' without reinforcements getting called in.	15	Bronze
	Choppers Down	Shoot down 15 helicopters in 'Tank.'	15	Bronze
	Invisible Descent	Get to the server room in 'Bunker' without reinforcements getting called in.	15	Bronze

MISCELLANEOUS

Name	Description	Xbox 360 Gamer Points	PS3 Trophy Type
Secret Servers	Destroy all the servers in 'Archives' within 40 secs of the first being damaged.	10	Bronze
Haven't Got Nine Minutes	Complete 'Airfield' in under 4:35 (007 Classic difficulty).	15	Silver
Welcome to Russia	Make the initial rendezvous with 006 in 'Dam.'	5	Bronze
Made you feel it, did he?	Single Player: Silently subdue 30 enemies.	10	Bronze
Master at Arms	Single Player: Make a kill with every weapon.	10	Bronze
Dance Commander	Surrender to the music in 'Nightclub.'	5	Bronze

SPEED RUNS

Name	Description	Xbox 360 Gamer Points	PS3 Trophy Type
Get to the Chopper	Complete 'Carrier' in under 11:00 (007 difficulty or higher).	15	Silver
Russian Escape	Complete 'Archives' in under 15:10 (Agent difficulty or higher).	15	Silver
Solar Agitated	Complete 'Solar' in under 13:00 (007 Classic difficulty).	15	Silver

MULTIPLAYER

Name	Description	Xbox 360 Gamer Points	PS3 Trophy Type
Orbis Non Sufficit	Public Match: Complete a match on every map.	15	Bronze
Butter Hook	Public Match: As Tee Hee, get the most kills with a melee strike (min. 3 melee kills).	15	Bronze
Au-ned	Public Match: Achieve 79 kills with the Golden Gun in Golden Gun mode.	30	Bronze

	Name	Description	Xbox 360 Gamer Points	PS3 Trophy Type
	Clobbering	Public Match: Achieve 64 melee kills with the KL-033 Mk2.	30	Bronze
	Cheated	Public Match: Get killed the most times by Oddjob's hat (min. 3 deaths).	3	Bronze
	Hat Trick	Public Match: In one life, make three kills with Oddjob's hat.	20	Bronze
	Braced for Impact	Public Match: As Jaws, survive a shot to the head which would otherwise have killed you.	15	Bronze
	The Man Who Cannot Die	Public Match: As Baron Samedi, survive a bullet which would otherwise have killed you.	15	Bronze
	Console Compliancy	Public Match: Capture and defend the most consoles in one match of GoldenEye mode.	30	Bronze
	For England, Alec	Public Match: As Bond, kill 006 with an explosive device.	20	Bronze
	The Other Cheek	Public Match: As Bond, kill Zukovsky with a melee strike.	20	Bronze
	Full Deck	Public Match: Play at least one complete match of Classic Conflict with every character.	15	Bronze
	Boys with Toys	Public Match: Kill 50 enemies with Proximity Mines.	50	Bronze
	Lucky Seven	Public Match: Defuse a planted bomb which has exactly 0:07 seconds remaining on its fuse.	40	Bronze
	Boxing Clever	Public Match: Earn all accolades specific to Black Box.	30	Bronze
	Had Your Six	Public Match: Kill six enemies with the Wolfe .44 or Gold Plated Revolver without reloading.	30	Bronze

PLATINUM

	Name	Description	Xbox 360 Gamer Points	PS3 Trophy Type
	Reloaded	Unlock all Trophies.	N/A	Platinum

GOLDENEYE RELOADED 007

Tim Bogenn

DK/BradyGames, a division of Penguin Group (USA) Inc.
800 East 96th Street, 3rd Floor
Indianapolis, IN 46240

ISBN 10: 0-7440-1340-2

ISBN 13: 978-0-7440-1340-5

Printing Code: The rightmost double-digit number is the year of the book's printing; the rightmost single-digit number is the number of the book's printing. For example, 11-1 shows that the first printing of the book occurred in 2011.

14 13 12 11   4 3 2 1

Printed in the USA.

BRADYGAMES STAFF

PUBLISHER
Mike Degler

EDITOR-IN-CHIEF
H. Leigh Davis

TRADE & DIGITAL PUBLISHER
Brian Saliba

LICENSING MANAGER
Christian Sumner

OPERATIONS MANAGER
Stacey Beheler

CREDITS

DEVELOPMENT EDITOR
Jennifer Sims

BOOK DESIGNER
Ann-Marie Deets

PRODUCTION DESIGNERS
Tracy Wehmeyer
Jeff Weissenberger
Ashley Hardy